Company's Coming

Greatest Hits

Mexican

www.**company**scoming.com
visit our web-site

Over 175 best-selling recipes

GREATEST HITS SERIES

Mexican

First printing May 2001

Canadian Cataloguing in Publication Data
Paré, Jean
    Greatest hits: mexican

Issued also in French under title: Jean Paré grands
succès : mexicain.

(Greatest hits series)
Includes index.
ISBN 1-895455-57-X

    1. Cookery, Mexican. I. Title. II. Series: Paré, Jean
Greatest hits series.

TX716.M4M49 2001   641.5972   C00-901543-4

Published simultaneously in Canada
and the United States of America by
The Recipe Factory Inc. in conjunction with
Company's Coming Publishing Limited
2311 - 96 Street, Edmonton, Alberta,
Canada T6N 1G3
Tel: 780 • 450-6223
Fax: 780 • 450-1857
www.companyscoming.com

Company's Coming is a registered trademark owned
by Company's Coming Publishing Limited
Printed in Canada

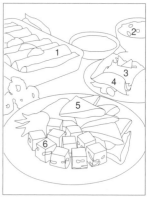

FRONT COVER:
1. Chicken Burritos, page 46
2. Bean And Corn Salsa, page 34
3. Taco Salad, page 60
4. Tortilla Bowls, page 59
5. Quesadilla Starters, page 22
6. Chilies Rellenos Squares,
   page 25

Props Courtesy Of: The Bay

www.**companys**coming.com
visit our web-site

table of contents

our cookbooks

COMPANY'S COMING SERIES

150 Delicious Squares
Appetizers
Appliance Cooking
Breads
Breakfasts & Brunches
Cakes
Casseroles
Chicken, Etc.
Cook For Kids NEW
Cookies
Cooking for Two
Desserts
Dinners of the World
Kids Cooking
Light Casseroles
Light Recipes
Low-Fat Cooking
Low-Fat Pasta
Main Courses
Make-Ahead Meals
Meatless Cooking
Muffins & More
One-Dish Meals
Pasta
Pies
Pizza!
Preserves
Salads
Slow Cooker Recipes
Soups & Sandwiches
Starters
Stir-Fry
The Potato Book
Vegetables

GREATEST HITS

Biscuits, Muffins & Loaves
Dips, Spreads & Dressings
Italian
Mexican
Soups & Salads
Sandwiches & Wraps

LIFESTYLE SERIES

Diabetic Cooking
Grilling
Low-fat Cooking
Low-fat Pasta

SPECIAL OCCASIONS SERIES

Chocolate Everything

company's coming story

ean Paré grew up understanding that the combination of family, friends and home cooking is the essence of a good life. From her mother she learned to appreciate good cooking, while her father praised even her earliest attempts. When she left home she took with her many acquired family recipes, a love of cooking and an intriguing desire to read recipe books like novels!

In 1963, when her four children had all reached school age, Jean volunteered to cater the 50th anniversary of the Vermilion School of Agriculture, now Lakeland College. Working out of her home, Jean prepared a dinner for over 1000 people which launched a flourishing catering operation that continued for over eighteen years. During that time she was provided with countless opportunities to test new ideas with immediate feedback—resulting in empty plates and contented customers! Whether preparing cocktail sandwiches for a house party or serving a hot meal for 1500 people, Jean Paré earned a reputation for good food, courteous service and reasonable prices.

"Why don't you write a cookbook?" Time and again, as requests for her recipes mounted, Jean was asked that question. Jean's response was to team up with her son, Grant Lovig, in the fall of 1980 to form Company's Coming Publishing Limited. April 14, 1981, marked the debut of "150 DELICIOUS SQUARES", the first Company's Coming cookbook in what soon would become Canada's most popular cookbook series.

Jean Paré's operation has grown steadily from the early days of working out of a spare bedroom in her home. Full-time staff includes marketing personnel located in major cities across Canada. Home Office is based in Edmonton, Alberta in a modern building constructed specially for the company.

Today the company distributes throughout Canada and the United States in addition to numerous overseas markets, all under the guidance of Jean's daughter, Gail Lovig. Best-sellers many times over, Company's Coming cookbooks are published in English and French, plus a Spanish-language edition is available in Mexico. Familiar and trusted in home kitchens the world over, Company's Coming cookbooks are offered in a variety of formats, including the original softcover series.

Jean Paré's approach to cooking has always called for quick and easy recipes using everyday ingredients. Even when traveling, she is constantly on the lookout for new ideas to share with her readers. At home, she can usually be found researching and writing recipes, or working in the company's test kitchen. Jean continues to gain new supporters by adhering to what she calls "the golden rule of cooking": never share a recipe you wouldn't use yourself. It's an approach that works—*millions of times over!*

foreword

hen you need a little spice in your life, do you reach for jalapeño peppers? Whether you're a fan of hot foods or prefer milder fares, Mexican provides over 150 recipes with a south-of-the-border flare.

Mexican cooking has taken its place at the table with easy-to-find ingredients, simple preparation and flavor to spare. The variety of uses for soft tortillas, fresh vegetables and tender meat provides an array of dishes. Start your day with zip by whipping up Egg Fajitas, Egg Enchiladas or Breakfast Burritos. How about Quesadillas for lunch, with Mexican Salad in your own Tortilla Bowls baked in the oven or microwave? Or Pinto Tortilla Soup with a slice of Taco Cornmeal Bread on the side.

If you're heading out to a party or throwing your own, rev up appetites with Green Chili Snacks or call out the fire trucks for Chilies Rellenos – a deep-fried, cheese-stuffed hot pepper. As an after-school or pre-game snack, Nacho Two Step or Chicken Nachos fit the bill, with Guacamole or Red-Onion Salsa on the side.

Looking for a great dip or spread? Refried Bean Dip served warm with tortilla chips, or Mint Papaya Salsa with barbecued chicken or pork chops turns ordinary into extraordinary.

Mexican wouldn't be complete without Tacos, but we've also included Tex Mex Pizza with a cornmeal crust and Spareribs Mole with a hint of cocoa. Choose Chick 'N' Chili Penne, Crab Enchiladas or Steak Fajitas for dinner, any of which you can adjust to your own taste with hot sauce.

With Mexican at your fingertips, you'll have an abundance of red hot recipes to choose from!

each recipe

has been analyzed using the most updated version of the Canadian Nutrient File from Health Canada, which is based upon the United States Department of Agriculture (USDA) Nutrient Data Base.

Margaret Ng, B.Sc. (Hon), M.A.
Registered Dietician

all about peppers

How hot is too hot?

While some varieties of peppers such as bell are sweet and mild, hot peppers — or chili peppers — can sear your tongue. What makes them feel so fireball hot? Chili peppers contain capsaicin (kap-SAY-ih-sin) or capsaicinoids (kap-SAY-ih-sin-oyds), a substance that has no smell or taste but is insoluble in water which is why drinking a glass of water won't put out the flames.

Capsaicinoids cause the mouth to burn, eyes to water and nose to run by reacting with pain sensors in the mouth and throat. This substance is found mostly in the ribs and seeds of peppers. Removing those parts reduces the heat of the pepper. Please note that wearing gloves is strongly recommended while handling peppers.

The heat of a chili pepper is gauged on the amount of capsaicinoids it contains. One measurement is the Scoville heat unit, which is obtained by taste tests, then diluted until no heat is tasted. Other chemical tests exist, but results are still often stated in Scoville heat units.

Pure capsaicin has 16 million Scoville heat units compared to bell peppers which have zero!

Habaneros, the hottest chili peppers, come in at 200,000 to 300,000 Scoville units. That's still plenty hot enough for most chili connoisseurs!

Unlike other spicy foods like mustard, ginger or black pepper, capsaicin desensitizes a person to the pain so they can eventually eat hotter chili peppers and foods. The most common hot chilies are serrano, jalapeño and poblano. The habanero is red or green and is considered very hot.

A member of the nightshade family, which includes potatoes and tomatoes, chili peppers are grown as an annual in colder climates and as a perennial near the equator. The mild ancho and mulato are two common types, along with the very hot Thai or searing Scotch Bonnet.

By comparison, bell peppers come in green, red, yellow and sometimes purple but have sweetness instead of zing. They are used in dried and ground form in paprika, a spice associated with Hungarian cooking. Some Hungarian paprika is labeled sweet or hot, depending on the sharpness acquired from the amount of seeds included.

A Comparison of Pepper Heat

Many pepper categories have numerous varieties, so there is a wide margin of pungency measured in Scoville heat units.

Habanero: 100,000 to 300,000

Scotch Bonnet: 100,000 to 250,000

Tabasco: 100,000 to 200,000

Thai: 50,000 to 100,000

Chipotle: 50,000 to 100,000

Cayenne: 20,000 to 60,000

Jalapeño: 1,500 to 50,000

Serrano: 10,000 to 23,000

Ancho: 1,000 to 2,000

Poblano: 1,000 to 1,500

Pepperoncini (pep-per-awn-CHEE-nee)*:* 100 to 500

Mulato: 0-100

Bell: 0

Putting out the fire

Because capsaicin is an oil, drinking water will only spread it around your mouth more, rather than dousing the flames. Sipping milk and rinsing it around the mouth, or eating yogurt, rice, bread, sweets or sugar to absorb the hot stuff, are better methods. You can also try drinking tomato juice or eating a fresh lemon or lime. Some people believe the acidity balances out the alkalinity of the capsaicin.

Healthy vegetable

Pound for pound, green and red bell peppers have twice and three times as much Vitamin C as citrus fruit respectively. Hot chili peppers can contain up to 350% more than an orange but the amount most people eat is minimal. Chili peppers also a good source of Vitamin E.

Buying

Chili peppers are growing in popularity, with approximately 7.5 million acres of various types of capsaicin grown in the world. This means that they are becoming more readily available in your local grocery store. Whether you're buying fresh or dried peppers, look for glossy, bright colors. Avoid peppers with soft spots or marks. Dried peppers should be uniform in color.

Storing

Store fresh peppers in the refrigerator for up to a week in a paper bag or vegetable drawer. Do not wash beforehand. Do not store with apples, pears or tomatoes, since these fruits produce ethylene, a substance which hastens the aging of peppers.

To freeze hot peppers, broil or blanch for 3 minutes, peel and place in freezer storage bag.

Dried chilies should be stored in an airtight container in a dark, dry, cool location.

Paprika should be stored in an airtight container in the refrigerator to retain flavor, color and nutritional value.

Hot pepper sauce can be stored indefinitely in the refrigerator.

Roasting

For wonderful flavor, try roasting peppers for use in your favorite recipes. Place bell peppers or chili peppers in a broiler pan. Broil 4 inches (10 cm) from heat, turning occasionally until peppers are charred and blistered in places. Remove peppers to a bowl. Cover with plastic wrap. Let sweat for about 15 minutes until cool enough to handle. Remove and discard skin from peepers by scraping with a knife.

mexican party planner

If you want to impress all the señors and señoritas you know, a Mexican party is easy to plan and sure to get everyone into the spirit of the moment.

Decorations: Collect sombreros, Mexican shawls and blankets from friends, family and thrift stores. Sombreros are great for a Mexican hat dance, or tossing nacho chips into for a game – the person who can hit the hat from the furthest away wins! Also be on the lookout for gourd maracas, anything with a hot chili pepper motif, and colorful crêpe paper flowers. Streamers and balloons in red, white and green (the colors of the Mexican flag) are also great ways to set the mood.

For authenticity, plan a Cinco de Mayo fiesta, to celebrate May 5, 1862 when the small, poorly equipped Mexicans defeated the larger, more modern French army in battle in the state of Puebla. Send out invitations in bandanas or with a jalapeño pepper attached.

Menu (for 20 people)

Serve a buffet-style feast so everyone can sample the variety found in Mexican foods.
Choose from the following:

Appetizers

Tortilla Roll-Ups, page 15	Cuts into 27 pieces
Green Chili Bits, page 16	Cuts into 36
Chili Cheese Log, page 21	Makes 2 rolls
Chili Con Queso (1), page 23	Makes 3 cups
Taco Dip, page 29	Makes 3 cups
Guacamole (1), page 14	Makes 2 cups
(Serve with a variety of crackers and colored tortilla chips)	

Beverages

Margaritas, page 31 (Easily doubled or tripled)	Makes 1 drink
Grapefruit Punch, page 32	Makes 12 cups
Mai Tai, page 32 (Easily doubled or tripled)	Makes 1 drink

Soups

Spicy Beef And Rice Soup, page 69	Makes 10 cups
Pinto Tortilla Soup, page 65	Makes 8½ cups

Salads

Mexican Salad, page 58 (Easily doubled or tripled)	Serves 4
Basil Cream Fiesta, page 64	Makes 10 cups

Main Dishes

Taco On A Platter, page 47	Serves 12
Serve with Sassy Salsa, page 40	Makes 3 pint (500 mL) jars
Taco Cornmeal Bread, page 49	Makes 2 loaves
Chili Mole, page 75 (Easily doubled)	Serves 6
Chicken Fajita Pasta, page 79 (Easily doubled)	Serves 6
Corny Beef Enchiladas, page 99 (Easily doubled or tripled)	Serves 4

Dessert

Margaritagrill	Serves 6
Fresh Fruit Quesadillas, page 114	Cuts into 16 wedges
Mango Fluff, page 113	Serves 8

★★★★★★★★★★★★★★★★★★★★★★★★★★★★★★★★★★

Music: Your local library is a good place to look for Mexican music. If they don't have anything on file, ordering from another branch is possible. Of course, music stores may carry some music that makes people shake a maraca — ask for movie soundtracks with a Spanish theme.

Piñatas: A Mexican party isn't complete without a piñata. Dating back to the 16th century in Italy, the piñata was once called a "pignatta." A blindfolded person would take a swing at the pignatta which was suspended by a rope. When it broke, guests rushed for the candy, trinkets and jewelry inside. The custom spread throughout Europe and Spanish explorers brought it to America where Mexicans adopted it as their own. Mexican artists used their creative skills to make piñatas out of papier maché, cardboard, paper and paint.

Make Your Own Piñata:

Supplies:

- Large balloon
- Newspaper
- Papier maché glue (or flour mixed with water to make pancake batter consistency)
- Strong string
- Wrapped candies, trinkets, party favors
- Paint

Instructions:

- Blow up the balloon.
- Tear newspaper into 2 inch (5 cm) wide strips. Dip strips into glue and lay over balloon, criss-crossing each other for three layers. Leave small hole at knot to burst balloon and insert candies when dry.
- Cut string long enough to go around balloon, with enough left at both ends for tying and hanging from ceiling. Drape over balloon. With another piece the same length, drape over balloon at a right angle to the first piece of string. Cover with more newspaper strips dipped in glue. When finished, there should be six layers of paper.
- Dry completely (about 24 hours).
- Pop balloon and remove through hole.
- Fill with candies and other goodies.
- Close hole with masking tape or more newspaper strips.
- Paint and decorate, using colored paper and streamers.

When ready to set up, attach securely to ceiling with rope or bungee cord, about 2 feet higher than the tallest participant, in an area wide enough to swing a stick safely. Blindfold one participant at a time. Turn them around three times and hand them the stick. After they hit the piñata once (or twice or three times — it's up to you to decide), the next person takes a turn. When the piñata breaks, the participant may take off their mask and try to grab candy along with the onlookers.

Appetizers

Served at parties and as late-night snacks, these Mexican appetizers are sure to please! With chips, salsa, dips and other nibblies, there are plenty of choices to tame a rumbling stomach. Roll up Tortilla Pinwheels, page 15, and Green Chili Bites, page 16, as pretty snacks for your gang. Or put a Chili Cheese Log, page 21, and Jalapeño Jelly, page 30, out for guests with a variety of crackers and chips.

EMPANADAS

You may want to add more hot pepper sauce to these.

Cooking oil	2 tbsp.	30 mL
Finely chopped onion	1 cup	250 mL
Small green pepper, chopped	1	1
Lean ground beef	½ lb.	225 g
Can of tomatoes, drained and mashed	14 oz.	398 mL
Chopped raisins	2 tbsp.	30 mL
Chopped pitted ripe (or green)	2 tbsp.	30 mL
Salt	½ tsp.	2 mL
Worcestershire sauce	2 tsp.	10 mL
Hot pepper sauce	¼ tsp.	1 mL
Large hard-boiled egg, chopped	1	1
Pastry, your own or a mix, enough for 4 crusts		
Large egg, fork-beaten	**1**	**1**

Heat cooking oil in frying pan. Add onion, green pepper and ground beef. Sauté until onion is soft and beef is no longer pink. Drain.

Add next 6 ingredients. Simmer, stirring often, for 4 to 5 minutes. Remove from heat. Cool.

Add chopped egg. Stir. Makes 2¼ cups (550 mL) filling.

Roll out pastry on lightly floured surface. Cut into 3 inch (7.5 cm) circles. Put about 1 tsp. (5 mL) filling in center of each. Dampen edge halfway around with beaten egg. Fold over. Seal with fork. Cut small slit in top. Arrange on ungreased baking sheet. Bake in 400°F (205°C) oven for about 15 minutes until browned. Makes about 90 empanadas.

1 empanada: 53 Calories; 3.6 g Total Fat; 74 mg Sodium; 1 g Protein; 4 g Carbohydrate; trace Dietary Fiber

Pictured on page 17.

★★★★★★★★★★★★★★★★★★★★★★★★★★★★★★★★★

Mexican

GREEN CHILI SNACKS

A simple, delicious one-bowl recipe. Serve warm, or make ahead and serve cold. These freeze well.

Creamed cottage cheese	1 cup	250 mL
All-purpose flour	⅓ cup	75 mL
Baking powder	½ tsp.	2 mL
Baking soda	½ tsp.	2 mL
Salt	½ tsp.	2 mL
Large eggs	4	4
Margarine (or butter)	3 tbsp.	50 mL
Grated sharp Cheddar cheese	1½ cups	375 mL
Can of diced green chilies, drained	4 oz.	114 mL

Put first 7 ingredients into medium bowl. Beat on medium until well mixed.

Stir in cheese and green chilies. Turn into greased 8 x 8 inch (20 x 20 cm) baking dish. Bake in 350°F (175°C) oven for 45 to 55 minutes. Cuts into 25 pieces.

1 piece: 68 Calories; 4.7 g Total Fat; 193 mg Sodium; 4 g Protein; 2 g Carbohydrate; trace Dietary Fiber

Pictured on page 18.

CHILIES RELLENOS

Listed below are two methods of deep-frying these stuffed-pepper appetizers. Serve hot with Quick Tomato Sauce, this page.

Cans of whole green chilies (4 oz., 114 mL, each), drained	2	2
Monterey Jack cheese strips, cut to fit inside chilies	6	6
Large eggs, separated	6	6
All-purpose flour	½ cup	125 mL

All-purpose flour, for coating
Cooking oil, for deep-frying

Cut slit in chilies. Insert strip of cheese carefully in each.

Beat egg whites in medium bowl until stiff. Fold in egg yolks and first amount of flour.

Coat chili with second amount of flour. Dip into egg batter. Deep-fry in 375°F (190°C) cooking oil for 2 to 3 minutes per side until browned. Remove with slotted spoon to paper towel to drain. Makes 6 appetizers.

1 appetizer: 207 Calories; 11.8 g Total Fat; 141 mg Sodium; 12 g Protein; 13 g Carbohydrate; 1 g Dietary Fiber

QUICK TOMATO SAUCE

Use with Chilies Rellenos, this page.

Beef bouillon cube	⅕ oz.	6 g
Boiling water	1 cup	250 mL
Margarine (or butter)	3 tbsp.	50 mL
All-purpose flour	3 tbsp.	50 mL
Can of tomato sauce	7½ oz.	213 mL

Place bouillon cube in boiling water. Stir until dissolved. Set aside.

Melt margarine in small saucepan. Stir in flour. Add tomato sauce and beef bouillon. Heat and stir until boiling and thickened. Makes 2 cups (500 mL).

2 tbsp. (30 mL): 29 Calories; 2.8 g Total Fat; 204 mg Sodium; trace Protein; 2 g Carbohydrate; trace Dietary Fiber

Guacamole

Whether made as a dip, sauce or spread, guacamole wins fans with its creamy texture and vibrant color from the avocado. With so many recipes to choose from, we've provided both a spicy and a mild version. Great with chips, fajitas and quesadillas!

GUACAMOLE

Serve with corn chips. Since this freezes well, make it when ripe avocados are available.

Ripe avocados, peeled, pitted and cut up	4	4
Lemon juice	¼ cup	60 mL
Salad dressing (or mayonnaise)	½ cup	125 mL
Chopped onion	¼ cup	60 mL
Chili powder	1 tsp.	5 mL
Garlic powder	½ tsp.	2 mL
Salt	1 tsp.	5 mL
Pepper	¼ tsp.	1 mL
Cayenne pepper	¼ tsp.	1 mL
Medium tomatoes, seeded and diced	2	2

Put first 9 ingredients into blender. Process until smooth. Turn into small bowl. May be frozen at this point. Thaw well before using.

Stir in tomato. Makes about 3 cups (750 mL).

2 tbsp. (30 mL): 121 Calories; 11.2 g Total Fat; 218 mg Sodium; 1 g Protein; 6 g Carbohydrate; 1 g Dietary Fiber

GUACAMOLE

Use with any of the fajita recipes, pages 83 - 86.

Ripe avocados, peeled, pitted and mashed	2	2
Medium tomato, seeded and finely diced	1	1
Lemon juice	2 tbsp.	30 mL
Finely chopped onion	2 tbsp.	30 mL
Salt	½ tsp.	2 mL

Combine all 5 ingredients in small bowl. Stir. Makes about 1 cup (250 mL).

2 tbsp. (30 mL): 83 Calories; 7.5 g Total Fat; 169 mg Sodium; 1 g Protein; 5 g Carbohydrate; 1 g Dietary Fiber

Pictured on page 36.

Variation: Stir in ½ tsp. (2 mL) chili powder.

★★★★★★★★★★★★★★★★★★★★★★★★★★★★★★

TORTILLA PINWHEELS

Nifty little rolls.

Low-fat creamed cottage cheese	2 cups	500 mL
Margarine (or butter)	¼ cup	60 mL
Milk	2 tbsp.	30 mL
Lemon juice	1 tbsp.	15 mL
Chopped green onion	½ cup	125 mL
Can of diced green chilies, drained	4 oz.	113 g
Grated medium Cheddar cheese	1 cup	250 mL
Garlic salt	¼ tsp.	1 mL
Flour tortillas (8 inch, 20 cm, size), See Tip, page 85	12	12

Place first 4 ingredients in blender. Process until smooth. Turn into medium bowl.

Add onion, green chilies, cheese and garlic salt. Stir.

Spread ¼ cup (60 mL) cottage cheese mixture on each tortilla. Roll up tightly. Wrap in plastic wrap, sealing ends. Chill for at least 2 hours. Cut into ½ to ¾ inch (12 to 20 mm) slices. Makes about 12 dozen pinwheels.

1 pinwheel: 18 Calories; 0.7 g Total Fat; 37 mg Sodium; 1 g Protein; 2 g Carbohydrate; trace Dietary Fiber

Pictured on page 17.

TORTILLA ROLL-UPS

And some more nifty little rolls.

Light cream cheese, softened	4 oz.	125 g
Light salad dressing (or mayonnaise)	2 tbsp.	30 mL
Dijon mustard	2 tsp.	10 mL
Finely chopped dill pickle, drained	¼ cup	60 mL
Flour tortillas (10 inch, 25 cm, size)	3	3
Deli shaved beef (or finely chopped cooked roast beef)	8 oz.	225 g

Combine cream cheese, salad dressing and mustard in small bowl. Mix until smooth. Add pickles. Mix well.

Spread cheese mixture on tortillas to edges.

Lay beef on cheese mixture. Roll up tortillas tightly. Wrap in plastic wrap, sealing ends. Chill for at least 1 hour or overnight. Cut into 1 inch (2.5 cm) pieces. Skewer with cocktail or wooden picks. Makes 27 roll-ups.

1 roll-up: 46 Calories; 1.2 g Total Fat; 89 mg Sodium; 4 g Protein; 3 g Carbohydrate; trace Dietary Fiber

Pictured on page 17.

BURRITO SNACKS

Adjust quantity of salsa and cheese to your liking.

Cooking oil	1 tsp.	5 mL
Lean ground beef	¾ lb.	340 g
Chopped onion	1 cup	250 mL
Can of refried beans	14 oz.	398 mL
Can of diced green chilies, with liquid	4 oz.	114 mL
Flour tortillas (10 inch, 25 cm, size), warmed, see Tip, page 85	8	8
Grated Monterey Jack cheese	1 cup	250 mL
Salsa	½ cup	125 mL

Heat frying pan or wok on medium-high. Add cooking oil. Add ground beef and onion. Stir-fry until beef is no longer pink. Drain.

Add refried beans and chilies with liquid. Stir-fry until hot.

Place ½ cup (125 mL) beef mixture on each warmed tortilla. Spread bean mixture to within 1 inch (2.5 cm) of edges. Add cheese and salsa. Roll up, tucking in ends. Makes 8 burritos.

1 burrito: 366 Calories; 10 g Total Fat; 936 mg Sodium; 21 g Protein; 47 g Carbohydrate; 4 g Dietary Fiber

GREEN CHILI BITES

This really is yummy. Both spicy-hot and oven-hot.

Large eggs	5	5
All-purpose flour	¼ cup	60 mL
Baking powder	½ tsp.	2 mL
Salt	¼ tsp.	1 mL
Pepper	⅛ tsp.	0.5 mL
Margarine (or butter), melted	¼ cup	60 mL
Can of diced green chilies, drained	4 oz.	114 mL
Grated Monterey Jack cheese	2 cups	500 mL
Creamed cottage cheese, mashed with fork	1 cup	250 mL
Hot pepper sauce	¼ tsp.	1 mL

Beat eggs in medium bowl until frothy. Add flour, baking powder, salt, pepper and margarine. Beat well.

Stir in green chilies, Monterey Jack cheese, cottage cheese and hot pepper sauce. Pour into greased 9 x 9 inch (22 x 22 cm) baking dish. Bake in 350°F (175°C) oven for 35 to 45 minutes until lightly browned and set. Serve hot. Cuts into 36 squares.

1 square: 56 Calories; 4.2 g Total Fat; 126 mg Sodium; 3 g Protein; 1 g Carbohydrate; trace Dietary Fiber

1. Mexican Snackies, page 22
2. Tortilla Roll-Ups, page 15
3. Tortilla Pinwheels, page 15
4. Empanadas, page 12
5. Mexican Mini Quiches, page 21

Props Courtesy Of: Treasure Barrel

NACHOS

For a mild nacho, make this without the chilies or keep them in for a robust flavor. Use one or both cheeses. Do not freeze.

Tortilla chips	2 oz.	57 g
Grated mild or medium Cheddar cheese	⅓ cup	75 mL
Grated Monterey Jack cheese	⅓ cup	75 mL
Green onion, thinly sliced	1	1
Green (or pitted ripe) olives, sliced	4	4
Diced green chilies (or jalapeño peppers, canned or fresh), optional		
Salsa (optional)	¼ cup	60 mL
Sour cream (optional)	¼ cup	60 mL

Preheat oven to 350°F (175°C). Crowd tortilla chips on ungreased baking sheet.

Sprinkle with both cheeses, green onion, olives and chilies. Bake on center rack in oven for about 3 minutes to melt cheese.

Serve with salsa and/or sour cream. Serves 2.

1 serving: 339 Calories; 23.2 g Total Fat; 607 mg Sodium; 13 g Protein; 21 g Carbohydrate; 1 g Dietary Fiber

NACHO TWO STEP

This is worth hurrying home from school to make.

Tortilla chips	8 oz.	225 g
Medium tomatoes, seeded and diced	2	2
Can of diced green chilies, drained	4 oz.	114 mL
Sliced green onion	¼ cup	60 mL
Chili powder	½ tsp.	2 mL
Grated mild or medium Cheddar cheese	¼ cup	60 mL
Grated Monterey Jack cheese	2 cups	500 mL

Preheat oven to 350°F (175°C). Crowd tortilla chips on ungreased baking sheet.

Combine tomato, chilies, onion, chili powder and Cheddar cheese in medium bowl. Spoon over chips.

Sprinkle Monterey Jack cheese over top. Bake on center rack in oven for about 10 minutes until hot and cheese is melted. Serves 6.

1 serving: 384 Calories; 24.6 g Total Fat; 252 mg Sodium; 14 g Protein; 28 g Carbohydrate; 1 g Dietary Fiber

Clean baked cheese from dishes by scraping with a spatula. Run under very hot water and scrub with a brush or spatula. A dishwasher will take care of anything left that elbow grease doesn't.

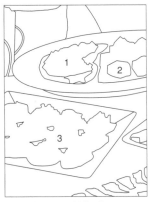

1. Salsa Dip, page 38
2. Green Chili Snacks, page 13
3. Tostaditos, page 25

Props Courtesy Of: Le Gnome
Stokes
The Basket House

NACHOS

Make NAH-chohs using the variations below.

Corn chips	4 cups	1 L
Grated mild Cheddar (or Monterey Jack) cheese	1 cup	250 mL
Bacon slices, cooked crisp and crumbled (or imitation bacon bits)	4	4
Green onions, chopped	4	4

Crowd corn chips on ungreased baking sheet. Sprinkle cheese over chips. Top with bacon and green onion. Bake in 350°F (175°C) oven for 10 minutes until hot and cheese is melted. Serves 4.

1 serving: 476 Calories; 30.2 g Total Fat; 729 mg Sodium; 14 g Protein; 37 g Carbohydrate; 3 g Dietary Fiber

Variations:

Grated Cheddar cheese, salsa, green onion

Grated Cheddar cheese, sliced olives, pepperoni slices

Refried beans, grated Cheddar cheese, sour cream

Tomato paste, grated Cheddar cheese, jalapeño slices

Salsa, grated Cheddar cheese

Grated Cheddar cheese, jalapeño slices

Chili con carne, grated Cheddar cheese

Refried beans, grated Cheddar cheese, jalapeño slices

CHICKEN NACHOS

You will enjoy these as an appetizer or as finger food.

Tortilla shells (10 inch, 25 cm, size)	6	6
Cooked shredded chicken	1½ cups	375 mL
Salsa	6 tbsp.	100 mL
Pitted ripe olives, sliced	6	6
Green onions, chopped	6	6
Sour cream	¾ cup	175 mL
Grated Monterey Jack (or mozzarella) cheese	1½ cups	375 mL
Canned jalapeño pepper slices	24	24

Place tortilla shells on ungreased baking sheet. Divide chicken among tortillas. Spread to within 1 inch (2.5 cm) of edges. Dab 1 tbsp. (15 mL) salsa on each tortilla. Sprinkle with olives and onion. Put 2 tbsp. (30 mL) sour cream and ¼ cup (60 mL) cheese on each. Bake in 400°F (205°C) oven for 20 minutes until hot and cheese is melted. Cut into quarters to serve.

Top each quarter with jalapeño slice. Makes 24 appetizers.

1 appetizer: 94 Calories; 4.3 g Total Fat; 157 mg Sodium; 6 g Protein; 8 g Carbohydrate; 1 g Dietary Fiber

MEXICAN MINI QUICHE

The green chilies add the special flavor to these.

Pastry, your own or a mix, enough for 2 crusts

Can of diced green chilies	4 oz.	113 g
Chopped onion	¼ cup	60 mL
Large eggs	2	2
Salad dressing (or mayonnaise)	½ cup	125 mL
Grated Monterey Jack cheese	½ cup	125 mL
Grated medium Cheddar cheese	½ cup	125 mL
Milk	⅓ cup	75 mL
Salt	¼ tsp.	1 mL
Pimiento pieces	**42**	**42**

Roll pastry fairly thin. Cut to fit small tart tins. Line tins.

Place next 8 ingredients in blender. Process until fairly smooth. Fill shells ¾ full. Bake on bottom rack in 400°F (205°C) oven for 12 to 15 minutes until set.

Garnish with pimiento pieces. Makes about 3½ dozen mini quiches.

1 mini quiche: 76 Calories; 5.5 g Total Fat; 141 mg Sodium; 2 g Protein; 5 g Carbohydrate; trace Dietary Fiber

Pictured on page 17.

CHILI CHEESE LOG

You will need to make this three or four days ahead to allow flavors to blend. Serve slices on round crackers, or leave log whole and serve with an assortment of crackers.

Grated medium Cheddar cheese	3 cups	750 mL
Cream cheese, softened	4 oz.	125 g
Worcestershire sauce	¾ tsp.	4 mL
Garlic salt	½ tsp.	2 mL
Pepper	¼ tsp.	1 mL
Chili powder	**lots**	

Put Cheddar cheese, cream cheese, Worcestershire sauce, garlic salt and pepper into medium bowl. Beat until soft and smooth. Divide in half. Shape into rolls a bit smaller than round cracker so slices will fit on top.

Sprinkle waxed paper liberally with chili powder. Roll each log to coat well. Wrap in waxed paper. Chill for 3 or 4 days. Freezes well. Makes 2 rolls. Each roll cuts into 24 slices, for a total of 48.

1 slice: 40 Calories; 3.4 g Total Fat; 72 mg Sodium; 2 g Protein; trace Carbohydrate; trace Dietary Fiber

Be careful not to burn cheese toppings when baking. Higher-fat cheeses, such as Cheddar, taste good when crispy and lightly browned. Low-fat cheeses can dry out and have a tougher texture if baked too long.

MEXICAN SNACKIES

Your guests will eat these up!

Biscuit mix	2 cups	500 mL
Chopped fresh cilantro (or ½ tsp., 2 mL, ground coriander)	¼ cup	60 mL
Water	½ cup	125 mL
Lean ground beef	½ lb.	225 g
Can of refried beans with green chilies	14 oz.	398 mL
Non-fat sour cream	1 cup	250 mL
Envelope of taco seasoning mix	1¼ oz.	35 g
Grated medium Cheddar cheese	1½ cups	375 mL
Finely chopped green onion	½ cup	125 mL
Finely chopped green pepper	¼ cup	60 mL
Finely chopped red pepper	¼ cup	60 mL
Seeded and finely diced tomato	1 cup	250 mL
Finely chopped pitted ripe olives	¼ cup	60 mL

Combine biscuit mix, cilantro and water in medium bowl. Stir to make a soft dough. Turn out on surface lightly coated with biscuit mix. Knead about 10 times. Press into ungreased 10 x 15 inch (25 x 38 cm) jelly roll pan. The dough will be very thin. Bake in 400°F (205°C) oven for 10 minutes until golden brown and firm. Cool.

Scramble-fry ground beef until no pink remains. Drain. Remove from heat. Stir in refried beans. Cool slightly. Spread on crust.

Combine sour cream and seasoning mix in small bowl. Spread on beef mixture. Sprinkle with cheese.

Combine remaining 5 ingredients in medium bowl. Sprinkle over cheese. Pack down slightly with hand. Chill for 1 hour. Cut into 1½ x 2 inch (3.8 x 5 cm) pieces. Makes 40 appetizers.

1 appetizer: 79 Calories; 3.3 g Total Fat; 264 mg Sodium; 4 g Protein; 9 g Carbohydrate; trace Dietary Fiber

Pictured on page 17.

QUESADILLA STARTERS

Here's an appetizer that doesn't crumble when you bite into it. Good hot or cold. Prepare in the morning. Brown when ready to serve. Do not freeze.

Grated Monterey Jack cheese	2 cups	500 mL
Flour tortillas (8 inch, 20 cm, size), warmed (see Tip, page 85)	6	6
Can of diced green chilies, drained	4 oz.	114 mL
Finely chopped onion	⅓ cup	75 mL
Medium avocado, peeled, seeded and chopped (optional)	1	1
Large tomato, finely diced	1	1
Cooking oil	2 tbsp.	30 mL

Scatter ⅓ cup (75 mL) cheese over half of each tortilla. Divide green chilies, onion, avocado and tomato among warmed tortillas. Moisten edges with water. Fold tortilla over filled half. Press edges with fork to seal. Cover with damp towel to keep moist.

Heat 1 tbsp. (15 mL) cooking oil in frying pan. Add 3 folded tortillas. Brown each side slowly for 3 minutes until cheese is melted. Repeat with remaining 3 tortillas. Cut each into 4 wedges, for a total of 24 wedges.

1 wedge: 92 Calories; 5.6 g Total Fat; 89 mg Sodium; 4 g Protein; 7 g Carbohydrate; trace Dietary Fiber

Pictured on front cover.

Chili Con Queso

Why settle for just one version, when all three of these recipes are great? Make each and serve them with a big bowl of nacho chips to feed a crowd! We've included two cold recipes and one that's best served warm.

CHILI CON QUESO

CHILL-ee khan-KAY-soh is just as delicious with potato chips, tortilla chips or fresh veggies. Make a day ahead to allow flavors to blend.

Finely chopped green pepper	¼ cup	60 mL
Process cheese loaf (such as Velveeta), cut into chunks	1 lb.	454 g
Light cream	¾ cup	175 mL
Can of diced green chilies, with liquid	4 oz.	114 mL
Chopped pimiento	4 tsp.	20 mL

Microwave green pepper for 2 minutes on high (100%) or boil in water in small saucepan until tender-crisp.

Put cheese, cream, chilies with liquid and pimiento into heavy saucepan or top of double boiler. Add green pepper. Heat on low, stirring often, until melted. If heated too fast or too hot, cheese may go stringy. Cool. Chill for 24 hours. Reheat to serve. Makes about 3 cups (750 mL).

2 tbsp. (30 mL): 70 Calories; 5.2 g Total Fat; 324 mg Sodium; 4 g Protein; 2 g Carbohydrate; trace Dietary Fiber

CHILI CON QUESO

Looks so inviting. For even more zip use Pepper Jack cheese in place of Monterey Jack. Keep hot in chafing dish or fondue pot.

Can of skim evaporated milk	13½ oz.	385 mL
All-purpose flour	3 tbsp.	50 mL
Can of stewed tomatoes, drained, chopped and drained again	14 oz.	398 mL
Can of diced green chilies, drained	4 oz.	114 mL
Chili powder	½ tsp.	2 mL
Garlic powder	⅛ tsp.	0.5 mL
Salt	½ tsp.	2 mL
Cayenne pepper	¼ tsp.	1 mL
Grated Monterey Jack cheese	3 cups	750 mL

Whisk evaporated milk into flour in large saucepan until smooth. Heat and stir until boiling and thickened.

Add remaining 7 ingredients, stirring often, until cheese is melted. Serve hot. Makes 4 cups (1 L).

2 tbsp. (30 mL): 56 Calories; 3.3 g Total Fat; 164 mg Sodium; 4 g Protein; 3 g Carbohydrate; trace Dietary Fiber

CHILI CON QUESO

It doesn't get any easier than this.

Process cheese loaf (such as Velveeta), cubed	1 lb.	454 g
Can of diced green chilies, with liquid	4 oz.	114 mL
Salsa	1¼ cups	300 mL

Combine cheese, chilies with liquid and salsa in 3½ quart (3.5 L) slow cooker. Stir. Cover. Cook on Low for 1½ hours, stirring occasionally, until quite warm. Makes a generous 3 cups (750 mL).

2 tbsp. (30 mL): 67 Calories; 4.5 g Total Fat; 516 mg Sodium; 4 g Protein; 3 g Carbohydrate; trace Dietary Fiber

Tortilla Chips

When making your own, you have a choice of deep-frying or baking.

Corn tortillas (6 inch, 15 cm, size)	12	12
Cooking oil, for deep-frying		
Salt (or seasoned salt), sprinkle		

Cut each tortilla into 8 wedges. Deep-fry, several at a time, in 375°F (190°C) cooking oil, turning occasionally, until crisp. Remove with slotted spoon to paper towels to drain.

Sprinkle with salt. Makes 96 chips.

4 chips: 72 Calories; 3.8 g Total Fat; 35 mg Sodium; 1 g Protein; 9 g Carbohydrate; 1 g Dietary Fiber

Pictured on page 35.

OVEN TORTILLA CHIPS: Arrange wedges in single layer on ungreased baking sheets. Brush lightly with water. Sprinkle with salt. Bake in 400°F (205°C) oven for about 8 minutes. Turn wedges over. Bake for about 3 minutes.

Tortilla Stacks

Easy to serve on small plates in the living room before the call to the table. Delicious.

Lean ground beef	½ lb.	225 g
Finely chopped onion	½ cup	125 mL
Salsa	3 tbsp.	50 mL
Flour tortillas (10 inch, 25 cm, size)	3	3
Can of diced green chilies, drained	4 oz.	114 mL
Medium tomato, seeded and diced	1	1
Grated Monterey Jack cheese	⅓ cup	75 mL
Grated medium Cheddar cheese	⅓ cup	75 mL

Scramble-fry ground beef and onion in non-stick frying pan until beef is no longer pink and onion is soft. Drain.

Stir in salsa. Cool.

Lay 1 tortilla on greased baking sheet. Spread beef mixture on top. Cover with second tortilla. Sprinkle with green chilies. Top with third tortilla. Scatter with tomato.

Toss both cheeses together. Sprinkle over tomato. Bake in 425°F (220°C) oven for about 15 minutes. Cuts into 8 wedges.

1 wedge: 155 Calories; 5.8 g Total Fat; 318 mg Sodium; 10 g Protein; 15 g Carbohydrate; 1 g Dietary Fiber

Tortilla Crisps

Quick to make and very tasty. Serve with Mexican-type dips or enjoy them as they are.

Margarine (or butter), softened	¾ cup	175 mL
Grated Parmesan cheese	½ cup	125 mL
Parsley flakes	2 tsp.	10 mL
Sesame seeds	¼ cup	60 mL
Dried whole oregano	½ tsp.	2 mL
Onion powder	¼ tsp.	1 mL
Garlic powder	¼ tsp.	1 mL
Flour tortillas (6 inch, 15 cm, size)	12	12

Combine first 7 ingredients in medium bowl. Mix well.

Spread each tortilla with thick layer of cheese mixture. Cut each into 8 wedges. Arrange individually on ungreased baking sheets. Bake in 350°F (175°C) oven for 12 to 15 minutes until crisp and browned. Makes 96 crisps.

1 crisp: 32 Calories; 2 g Total Fat; 45 mg Sodium; 1 g Protein; 3 g Carbohydrate; trace Dietary Fiber

Pictured on page 35.

TOSTADAS

A toh-STAH-dah makes a tasty starter appetizer.

Flour tortillas (8 inch, 20 cm, size)	6	6
Cooking oil		
Refried beans (or ground beef, scramble-fried and drained), see Note	1 cup	250 mL
Salsa	6 tbsp.	100 mL
Grated Monterey Jack cheese	1 cup	250 mL
Shredded lettuce	2 cups	500 mL
Grated Cheddar cheese	½ cup	125 mL
Chopped green onion	2 tbsp.	30 mL

Fry tortillas in hot cooking oil in frying pan until crisp.

Divide remaining 6 ingredients, in order given, among tortillas. Makes 6 tostadas.

1 tostada: 303 Calories; 12.6 g Total Fat; 729 mg Sodium; 15 g Protein; 33 g Carbohydrate; 3 g Dietary Fiber

Note: Instead of using refried beans or ground beef, both may be used.

TOSTADITOS

Pretty little morsels of red, green and white. A taste of Mexico. Have all ingredients ready in the morning. Spread on chips just before serving so they don't get soggy.

Round tortilla chips	20	20
Can of jalapeño bean dip (or refried beans), heated	10½ oz.	298 mL
Sour cream	½ cup	125 mL
Salsa	½ cup	125 mL
Sliced green onion	2 tbsp.	30 mL
Grated Monterey Jack cheese	½ cup	125 mL

Arrange tortilla chips on ungreased baking sheet.

Spread layers on each as follows: 1 tbsp. (15 mL) bean dip, 1 tsp. (5 mL) sour cream, 1 tsp. (5 mL) salsa, ¼ tsp. (1 mL) green onion and 1 tsp. (5 mL) cheese. May be served as is or baked in 350°F (175°C) oven for about 5 minutes until cheese is melted. Makes 20 tostaditos.

1 tostadito: 68 Calories; 3.4 g Total Fat; 184 mg Sodium; 2 g Protein; 7 g Carbohydrate; 1 g Dietary Fiber

Pictured on page 18.

CHILIES RELLENOS SQUARES

Looks great. Tastes great. Easy to make.

Cans of whole green chilies (4 oz., 114 mL, each), drained, seeds removed	2	2
Monterey Jack cheese, grated	1 lb.	454 g
Large eggs	2	2
Sour cream	1 cup	250 mL
Salt	¼ tsp.	1 mL
Pepper	⅛ tsp.	0.5 mL

Cut chilies flat. Layer ½ in greased 8 x 8 inch (20 x 20 cm) baking dish. Layer with ½ of cheese. Repeat layers with remaining chilies and remaining cheese.

Beat eggs until frothy. Add sour cream, salt and pepper. Mix. Pour over cheese. Bake, uncovered, in 350°F (175°C) oven for 45 minutes until set. Cut into 1 inch (2.5 cm) squares. Makes 64 squares.

1 serving: 36 Calories; 2.8 g Total Fat; 94 mg Sodium; 2 g Protein; trace Carbohydrate; trace Dietary Fiber

Pictured on front cover.

TACO PIZZA SQUARES

One of those great appetizers that you can serve hot or cold — good either way.

Basic Pizza Crust dough, page 95	1	1
Can of refried beans with jalapeño peppers	14 oz.	398 mL
Non-fat sour cream	1 cup	250 mL
Salsa	¾ cup	175 mL
Grated Monterey Jack cheese	¾ cup	175 mL
Grated medium Cheddar cheese	¾ cup	175 mL
Green onions, chopped	2	2
Chopped pitted ripe olives	¼ cup	60 mL

Prepare pizza dough. Roll out until slightly larger than 9 x 13 inches (22 x 33 cm). Place in greased 9 x 13 inch (22 x 33 cm) baking dish, forming rim around edge. Poke holes all over with fork. Bake on center rack in 425°F (220°C) oven for 5 minutes. Press down any bulges with tea towel. Bake for about 5 minutes until fully cooked.

Spread refried beans on crust. Spread sour cream on refried beans. Drizzle with salsa.

Toss both cheeses together in small bowl. Sprinkle over salsa.

Scatter green onion and olives on top. Broil 6 inches (15 cm) from heat until cheese is melted, or bake on center rack in 425°F (220°C) oven for about 5 minutes until cheese is melted. Cuts into 24 squares.

1 square: 118 Calories; 4 g Total Fat; 287 mg Sodium; 5 g Protein; 16 g Carbohydrate; 2 g Dietary Fiber

MEXI DIP

When you dip into this with a sturdy chip or spoon, you get different layers.

Light cream cheese (8 oz., 250 g, each), softened	2	2
Can of ham flakes, with liquid, mashed	6½ oz.	184 g
Grated medium Cheddar cheese	3 cups	750 mL
Salsa	½ cup	125 mL
Can of diced green chilies, drained	4 oz.	114 mL
Chili powder	½-1 tsp.	2-5 mL

Mash cream cheese with fork in small bowl. Spread in bottom of 3½ quart (3.5 L) slow cooker.

Sprinkle ham with liquid evenly over top. Sprinkle with Cheddar cheese.

Stir salsa and green chilies together in small bowl. Spoon on top.

Sprinkle with chili powder. Cover. Cook on Low for 2 to 2½ hours until quite warm. Do not stir. Makes 4¼ cups (1 L).

2 tbsp. (30 mL): 90 Calories; 7.1 g Total Fat; 367 mg Sodium; 5 g Protein; 1 g Carbohydrate; trace Dietary Fiber

★★★★★★★★★★★★★★★★★★★★★★★★★★★★★★★★★★★★

BLACK BEAN DIP

A darkish dip with cheese sprinkled over top.
Cider vinegar gives it a good tang. Serve with
tortilla chips, corn chips or raw vegetables.

Can of black beans, drained and rinsed	19 oz.	540 mL
Apple cider vinegar	2 tsp.	10 mL
Salt	½ tsp.	2 mL
Pepper	⅛ tsp.	0.5 mL
Garlic powder	¼ tsp.	1 mL
Onion powder	¼ tsp.	1 mL
Hot pepper sauce (optional)	¼ tsp.	1 mL
TOPPING		
Grated medium Cheddar cheese	¼ cup	60 mL
Ground walnuts	1 tbsp.	15 mL

Mash beans well with fork on plate. Turn into small bowl.

Add next 6 ingredients. Stir. Transfer to serving dish.

Topping: Sprinkle cheese and walnuts over top. Chill until needed. Makes 1⅓ cups (325 mL).

2 tbsp. (30 mL): 71 Calories; 1.5 g Total Fat; 254 mg Sodium; 5 g Protein; 10 g Carbohydrate; 2 g Dietary Fiber

MEXICAN BEAN DIP

No need to travel south to get a good dip.
Guests will devour this in no time. Serve with
assorted crackers.

Cream cheese, softened	8 oz.	250 g
Sour cream	1 cup	250 mL
Can of refried beans	14 oz.	398 mL
Onion flakes	1 tbsp.	15 mL
Chopped chives	1 tbsp.	15 mL
Parsley flakes	1 tbsp.	15 mL
Chili powder	2 tbsp.	30 mL
Grated medium or sharp Cheddar cheese	1½ cups	375 mL
Grated Monterey Jack cheese	1½ cups	375 mL
Chili powder	2 tbsp.	30 mL

Mix first 7 ingredients well in bowl. Spread in 3 quart (3 L) casserole.

Sprinkle with Cheddar cheese, then with Monterey Jack cheese. Sprinkle second amount of chili powder over top. May be chilled at this point until needed. Bake, uncovered, in 350°F (175°C) oven for about 20 minutes until hot. Makes 5 cups (1.25 L).

2 tbsp. (30 mL): 77 Calories; 5.9 g Total Fat; 121 mg Sodium; 4 g Protein; 3 g Carbohydrate; 1 g Dietary Fiber

KIDNEY BEAN DIP

If you're into spicy, you can add more cayenne pepper to this. Serve with tortilla chips, raw vegetables or corn chips.

BOTTOM LAYER

Cans of kidney beans (14 oz., 398 mL, each), drained	2	2
Salsa	6 tbsp.	100 mL
Sliced green onion	½ cup	125 mL
Chili powder	1 tsp.	5 mL
Onion powder	½ tsp.	2 mL
Garlic powder	¼ tsp.	1 mL
White vinegar	1 tsp.	5 mL
Parsley flakes	2 tsp.	10 mL
Salt	½ tsp.	2 mL
Cayenne pepper	¼ tsp.	1 mL

TOP LAYER

Grated medium Cheddar cheese	1 cup	250 mL
Grated Monterey Jack cheese	1 cup	250 mL
Chili powder	1 tsp.	5 mL

Bottom Layer: Mash kidney beans with fork in medium bowl.

Add next 9 ingredients. Mix well. Spread in ungreased 9 inch (22 cm) pie plate or shallow casserole.

Top Layer: Sprinkle with Cheddar cheese, then Monterey Jack cheese. Sprinkle with chili powder. Bake, uncovered, in 350°F (175°C) oven for about 30 minutes. Makes about 4 cups (1 L).

1 tbsp. (15 mL): 24 Calories; 1.2 g Total Fat; 79 mg Sodium; 2 g Protein; 2 g Carbohydrate; 1 g Dietary Fiber

GARBANZO DIP

Serve with crackers or Tortilla Crisps, page 24.

Cooking oil	2 tbsp.	30 mL
Chopped onion	1 cup	250 mL
Small green pepper, chopped	1	1
Chopped celery	⅓ cup	75 mL
Can of garbanzo beans (chick peas), drained and rinsed	14 oz.	398 mL
Lemon juice	4 tsp.	20 mL
Dried whole oregano	1 tsp.	5 mL
Garlic powder	¼ tsp.	1 mL
Salt	½ tsp.	2 mL
Pepper	⅛ tsp.	0.5 mL

Heat cooking oil in non-stick frying pan. Add onion, green pepper and celery. Sauté for 10 to 15 minutes until soft.

Combine remaining 6 ingredients in food processor or blender. Add onion mixture. Process until smooth. Makes 1¾ cups (425 mL).

1 tbsp. (15 mL): 24 Calories; 1.2 g Total Fat; 65 mg Sodium; 1 g Protein; 3 g Carbohydrate; trace Dietary Fiber

★★★★★★★★★★★★★★★★★★★★★★★★★★★★

REFRIED BEAN DIP

Serve this dip warm with tortilla chips.

Can of refried beans	14 oz.	398 mL
Salsa	1 cup	250 mL
Lean ground beef	1 lb.	454 g
Salt, to taste		
Grated medium Cheddar cheese	1 cup	250 mL
Non-fat sour cream	1 cup	250 mL
Finely chopped green onion	2 tbsp.	30 mL
Shredded iceberg lettuce	1 cup	250 mL
Medium tomato, seeded and chopped	1	1

Combine beans with 2 tsp. (10 mL) salsa. Spread evenly in ungreased 10 inch (25 cm) pie plate.

Scramble-fry ground beef in non-stick frying pan until no pink remains. Drain. Add ½ cup (125 mL) salsa and salt. Cook and stir for 5 minutes. Spread beef mixture evenly on beans. Sprinkle with Cheddar cheese. Bake in 350°F (175°C) oven for 15 minutes until cheese is melted and beans are hot. Cool for 10 minutes.

Spread with remaining salsa. Combine sour cream and onion in small bowl. Spread on salsa. Sprinkle with lettuce and tomato. Makes 4 cups (1 L).

2 tbsp. (30 mL): 56 Calories; 2.6 g Total Fat; 96 mg Sodium; 5 g Protein; 4 g Carbohydrate; trace Dietary Fiber

TACO DIP

Always popular. Serve with tortilla chips.

Can of jalapeño bean dip	10½ oz.	298 mL
Ripe avocados, peeled, pitted and mashed	3	3
Lemon juice	1 tsp.	5 mL
Garlic salt (or garlic powder)	1 tsp.	5 mL
Sour cream	1 cup	250 mL
Envelope of taco seasoning mix	1¼ oz.	35 g
Grated Monterey Jack cheese	1 cup	250 mL
Grated medium Cheddar cheese	1 cup	250 mL
Large tomatoes, seeded and diced, drained on paper towels	2	2
Green onions, thinly sliced	4	4

Spread bean dip in 12 inch (30 cm) pizza pan or 10 inch (25 cm) quiche dish.

Mash avocado, lemon juice and garlic salt with fork. Spread on bean dip.

Stir sour cream and taco seasoning in small bowl. Spread on avocado layer. Sprinkle with Monterey Jack cheese, Cheddar cheese, tomato and green onion, in order given. Makes 4 cups (1 L).

2 tbsp. (30 mL): 82 Calories; 6.2 g Total Fat; 256 mg Sodium; 3 g Protein; 4 g Carbohydrate; 1 g Dietary Fiber

HOT PEPPER JELLY

This makes a greenish-colored jelly. Use red peppers and red food coloring to make a orange-red color. Great over a block of cream cheese served with crackers.

Chopped green pepper	1½ cups	375 mL
Can of diced jalapeño peppers, drained	4 oz.	114 mL
White vinegar	1½ cups	375 mL
Granulated sugar	6½ cups	1.6 L
Bottle of liquid pectin	6 oz.	170 mL
Green food coloring (optional)		

Combine green pepper, jalapeño pepper and vinegar in blender. Process until smooth. Pour into large pot or Dutch oven.

Add sugar. Heat and stir on medium-high until sugar is dissolved. Bring to a boil. Boil for 3 minutes.

Stir in pectin. Return to a full rolling boil. Boil hard for 1 minute. Remove from heat. Skim off foam.

Add a bit of food coloring to make desired green. Pour into hot sterilized half-pint (250 mL) jars to within ¼ inch (6 mm) of top. Place sterilized metal lids on jars and screw metal bands on securely. For added assurance against spoilage, process in boiling water bath for 15 minutes. Makes 6 half-pint (250 mL) jars.

2 tbsp. (30 mL): 94 Calories; trace Total Fat; 8 mg Sodium; trace Protein; 24 g Carbohydrate; trace Dietary Fiber

JALAPEÑO JELLY

Hah-lah-PEH-nyoh jelly is different and a treat to eat with cream cheese on crackers

Can of diced jalapeño peppers	4 oz.	114 mL
Chopped red pepper	¾ cup	175 mL
White vinegar	1 cup	250 mL
Lemon juice	3 tbsp.	50 mL
Granulated sugar	5 cups	1.25 L
Bottle of liquid pectin (6 oz., 170 mL, size)	½	½

Put jalapeño and red pepper into blender. Add ½ of vinegar. Process until smooth. Pour into large saucepan. Add remaining vinegar, lemon juice and sugar. Bring to a boil, stirring often. Boil for 3 minutes. Add pectin. Stir. Return to full rolling boil. Boil for 1 minute. Remove from heat. Skim off foam. Pour into sterilized half-pint (250 mL) jars, to within ¼ inch (6 mm) of top. Place sterilized metal lids on jars and screw metal bands on securely. For added assurance against spoilage, process in boiling water bath for 15 minutes. Makes 4 half-pint (250 mL) jars.

2 tbsp. (30 mL): 108 Calories; trace Total Fat; 8 mg Sodium; trace Protein; 28 g Carbohydrate; trace Dietary Fiber

Pictured on page 35.

Since most recipes rarely call for a whole can of tomato paste, freeze the can for 30 minutes. Open both ends and push contents through with one loose end, slicing off only what you need. Freeze the rest of the contents in plastic wrap for future use.

Beverages

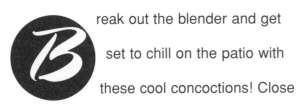

reak out the blender and get set to chill on the patio with these cool concoctions! Close your eyes while sipping on a salt-rimmed glass of tangy Margarita, page 31, or a creamy smooth Chi Chi, page 32, and you can almost hear the ocean breaking on the sand.

MARGARITA

A summer holiday drink. Try the variations as well.

Tequila	1½ oz.	45 mL
Triple Sec (or Cointreau)	½ oz.	15 mL
Lime juice	1 oz.	30 mL
Corn syrup	2-3 tsp.	10-15 mL
Crushed ice	½ cup	125 mL

Additional crushed ice (or ice cubes), to fill bowl-type glass

Combine first 5 ingredients in cocktail shaker. Shake well.

Strain over additional crushed ice in salt-rimmed glass. Makes 1 drink.

1 drink: 210 Calories; 0.1 g Total Fat; 11 mg Sodium; trace Protein; 20 g Carbohydrate; trace Dietary Fiber

STRAWBERRY MARGARITA: Omit lime juice. Add 10 frozen strawberries, cut up, to blender with Tequila, 1½ tbsp. (25 mL) corn syrup and crushed ice. Process until smooth. Pour over crushed ice in glass.

FROZEN MARGARITA: Process Tequila, Triple Sec, lime juice, corn syrup and 1½ cups (375 mL) crushed ice in blender until slushy.

CHI CHI

A creamy concoction to sip by the pool or on the deck.

Vodka	1½ oz.	45 mL
Thick coconut milk (or coconut cream)	2 tbsp.	30 mL
Pineapple juice	½ cup	125 mL
Crushed ice	1 cup	250 mL

Combine all 4 ingredients in blender. Process until smooth. Makes 1 drink.

1 drink: 244 Calories; 6.8 g Total Fat; 21 mg Sodium; 1 g Protein; 21 g Carbohydrate; 1 g Dietary Fiber

VIRGIN CHI CHI: Omit vodka. Add extra 3 tbsp. (50 mL) pineapple juice.

GRAPEFRUIT PUNCH

This is a good, refreshing drink. Not too sweet but just right.

Grapefruit juice (pink or white), chilled	4½ cups	1.1 L
Apple juice	3 cups	750 mL
Granulated sugar	1 cup	250 mL
Ginger ale	4½ cups	1.1 L
Ice cubes		

Stir grapefruit juice, apple juice and sugar together in medium bowl until sugar is dissolved. Chill until ready to use. Pour into punch bowl.

Add ginger ale. Stir gently. Add ice cubes. Makes about 12 cups (3 L).

1 cup (250 mL): 161 Calories; 0.2 g Total Fat; 9 mg Sodium; trace Protein; 40 g Carbohydrate; 1 g Dietary Fiber

MAI TAI

It is necessary to use all of these ingredients if you want to be a true Hawaiian wahini (wah-HEE-nee) or kane (KAH-nay). But you can imagine yourself on a warm Mexican beach too.

Crushed ice		
Light rum	¾ oz.	22 mL
Curaçao (or Triple Sec)	¼ oz.	8 mL
Lemon juice	3 tbsp.	50 mL
Pineapple juice	3 tbsp.	50 mL
Prepared orange juice	3 tbsp.	50 mL
Dark rum	¾ oz.	22 mL

Fill short tumbler with ice. Add light rum, Curaçao, lemon juice, pineapple juice and orange juice. Stir.

Float dark rum on top. Makes 1 drink.

1 drink: 197 Calories; 0.1 g Total Fat; 2 mg Sodium; 1 g Protein; 19 g Carbohydrate; trace Dietary Fiber

TEQUILA SUNRISE

If you watch closely, you will see the sunrise in this cocktail.

Ice cubes		
Tequila	**1½-2 oz.**	**45-60 mL**
Prepared orange juice, to fill		
Maraschino cherry, for garnish		
Orange slice, for garnish		
Grenadine syrup	**1-1½ tbsp.**	**15-25 mL**

Drop cubes into tall narrow glass. Add Tequila and orange juice. Stir.

Secure cherry and orange slice on rim of glass before adding grenadine.

Drop grenadine all at once into center of glass so it will fall to the bottom. It will rise, reminiscent of a sunrise. Makes 1 drink.

1 drink: 245 Calories; 0.1 g Total Fat; 17 mg Sodium; 1 g Protein; 36 g Carbohydrate; 1 g Dietary Fiber

PIÑA COLADA

A wonderful afternoon cocktail is creamy PEEN-yuh koh-LAH-duh. For fun, try serving it in a coconut shell.

Light rum	**1½ oz.**	**45 mL**
Thick coconut milk	**3 tbsp.**	**50 mL**
(or coconut cream)		
Pineapple (or other	**½ cup**	**125 mL**
tropical) juice		
Corn syrup	**1½ tbsp.**	**25 mL**
Crushed ice	**1 cup**	**250 mL**
(or small ice cubes)		

Combine all 5 ingredients in blender. Process well. Pour into large goblet. Makes 1 drink.

1 drink: 381 Calories; 10.1 g Total Fat; 54 mg Sodium; 2 g Protein; 49 g Carbohydrate; 1 g Dietary Fiber

VIRGIN PIÑA COLADA: Omit rum. Add extra 3 tbsp. (50 mL) pineapple juice.

MEXICAN HOT CHOCOLATE

Olé! This will soon become your favorite way to make hot chocolate.

Chocolate milk	**¾ cup**	**175 mL**
Ground cinnamon	**⅛ tsp.**	**0.5 mL**
Cocoa, sifted if lumpy	**1 tsp.**	**5 mL**
Whipped cream	**2 tbsp.**	**30 mL**
(or frozen whipped		
topping, thawed)		
Ground cinnamon, sprinkle		
Cinnamon stick	**1**	**1**

Heat milk in small saucepan on medium until very hot but not boiling. When making several drinks, use a heavy medium saucepan or double boiler.

Stir in cinnamon and cocoa. Pour into serving glass.

Top with whipped cream. Sift a light sprinkle of cinnamon over cream. Add cinnamon stick. Serves 1.

1 drink: 192 Calories; 9 g Total Fat; 125 mg Sodium; 7 g Protein; 22 g Carbohydrate; 2 g Dietary Fiber

Salsa

T his Mexican word for sauce translates into sweet and savory creations that are easy to make. Almost any dish is enhanced by one of these accompaniments. You couldn't ask for something better to add zing to plain chicken than Mint Papaya Salsa, page 38. Picante Salsa, page 39, is perfect on everything from eggs at breakfast to fajitas at dinner.

BEAN AND CORN SALSA

Serve with tortilla chips, or as a condiment with chicken or beef dishes. Try heating and serving over pasta. Chill, covered, for up to one week.

Chunky salsa	**1⅓ cups**	**325 mL**
Can of kernel corn, drained	**12 oz.**	**341 mL**
Can of black beans, drained (or 1 cup, 250 mL, cooked)	**14 oz.**	**398 mL**
Medium red onion, finely diced	**½**	**½**
Finely diced green or red pepper	**½ cup**	**125 mL**
Chili powder	**½ tsp.**	**2 mL**
Cayenne pepper, sprinkle		
Finely chopped fresh cilantro	**2 tbsp.**	**30 mL**

Combine all 8 ingredients in medium bowl. Let stand for about 30 minutes to blend flavors. Makes 5 cups (1.25 L).

¼ cup (60 mL): 36 Calories; 0.2 g Total Fat; 324 mg Sodium; 2 g Protein; 4 g Carbohydrate; 1 g Dietary Fiber

Pictured on front cover.

1. Guacamole Salad, page 62
2. Mint Papaya Salsa, page 38
3. Tortilla Crisps, page 24
4. Tortilla Chips, page 24
5. Jalapeño Jelly , page 30

★★★★★★★★★★★★★★★★★★★★★★★★★★★★★★★

RED ONION SALSA

Colorful and chunky. This is spicy hot and very good. A good go-with for protein dishes.

Large red onion, chopped	1	1
Medium red pepper, chopped	1	1
Red wine vinegar	¼ cup	60 mL
Instant vegetable stock mix	1 tbsp.	15 mL
Ground thyme	¼ tsp.	1 mL
Salt	½ tsp.	2 mL
Pepper	⅛ tsp.	0.5 mL
Cayenne pepper	⅛ tsp.	0.5 mL

Combine all 8 ingredients in small saucepan. Bring to a boil on medium. Boil gently, stirring occasionally, for about 20 minutes until thickened. Cool. Makes 1½ cups (375 mL).

2 tbsp. (30 mL): 12 Calories; 0.3 g Total Fat; 169 mg Sodium; trace Protein; 2 g Carbohydrate; trace Dietary Fiber

SALSA

Serve as a sauce or a dip for corn chips. Adjust the heat according to taste.

Cans of tomatoes (14 oz., 398 mL, each), with juice	2	2
Medium green pepper, cut into pieces	1	1
Chopped onion	½ cup	125 mL
Garlic powder (or 1 clove, minced)	¼ tsp.	1 mL
Salt	¼ tsp.	1 mL
Canned pickled jalapeño pepper slices	4	4

Put all 6 ingredients into blender. Process until smooth. Pour into saucepan. Bring to a boil. Reduce heat. Simmer slowly for 10 minutes. Chill. Makes 3 cups (750 mL).

2 tbsp. (30 mL): 9 Calories; 0.1 g Total Fat; 94 mg Sodium; trace Protein; 2 g Carbohydrate; trace Dietary Fiber

MEXICAN HOT SAUCE

For an authentic taste, add more dried red chilies.

Medium tomatoes, peeled and diced	3	3
Finely chopped onion	⅓ cup	75 mL
Chopped chives	1 tbsp.	15 mL
Parsley flakes	1 tsp.	5 mL
Dried crushed chilies	½ tsp.	2 mL
Salt, light sprinkle		
Granulated sugar	¼ tsp.	1 mL

Measure all 7 ingredients into small bowl. Stir to mix. Let stand for at least 30 minutes to allow flavors to blend. Makes about 1 cup (250 mL).

2 tbsp. (30 mL): 13 Calories; 0.2 g Total Fat; 6 mg Sodium; trace Protein; 3 g Carbohydrate; 1 g Dietary Fiber

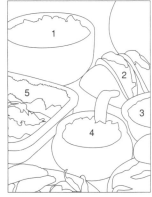

Props Courtesy Of: Le Gnome

SALSA DIP

Serve with tortilla chips for dipping. While this can be made ahead, do not freeze. Store in refrigerator.

Medium tomatoes, peeled, seeded and diced	3	3
Green onions, chopped	3	3
Can of diced green chilies, with liquid	4 oz.	113 mL
Chopped pitted ripe olives	¼ cup	60 mL
Cooking oil	2 tbsp.	30 mL
White vinegar	1½ tbsp.	25 mL
Garlic powder	½ tsp.	2 mL
Salt	½ tsp.	2 mL
Pepper	⅛ tsp.	0.5 mL

Combine all 9 ingredients in small bowl. Cover. Chill for at least 2 hours to allow flavors to blend. Makes 3 cups (750 mL).

2 tbsp. (30 mL): 15 Calories; 1.3 g Total Fat; 64 mg Sodium; trace Protein; 1 g Carbohydrate; trace Dietary Fiber

Pictured on page 18.

MINT PAPAYA SALSA

A great make-ahead for your next weekend barbecue bash. Keep a supply in the refrigerator for year-round indoor or outdoor grilling.

Ripe medium papayas, peeled, seeded and diced	2	2
Finely diced red onion	½ cup	125 mL
Chopped fresh mint leaves	¼ cup	60 mL
Lime juice	2 tsp.	10 mL
Salt	¼ tsp.	1 mL
Freshly ground pepper, sprinkle		

Combine all 6 ingredients in small bowl. Cover. Chill for at least 2 hours to allow flavors to blend. Can be stored in refrigerator for up to 5 days. Makes 3 cups (750 mL).

2 tbsp. (30 mL): 11 Calories; trace Total Fat; 28 mg Sodium; trace Protein; 3 g Carbohydrate; trace Dietary Fiber

Pictured on page 35.

SALSA

Tangy and hot. Make it hotter by adding more cayenne.

Cans of tomatoes (28 oz., 796 mL, each), with juice	2	2
Cans of tomato sauce (7½ oz., 213 mL, each)	2	2
Medium green peppers, chopped	2	2
Medium red pepper, chopped	1	1
Chopped onion	2 cups	500 mL
White vinegar	⅔ cup	150 mL
Granulated sugar	3 tbsp.	50 mL
Coarse (pickling) salt	2 tsp.	10 mL
Paprika	2 tsp.	10 mL
Garlic powder	½ tsp.	2 mL
Dried whole oregano	½ tsp.	2 mL
Cayenne pepper, to taste	¼-1 tsp.	1-5 mL

Measure all 12 ingredients into large saucepan. Bring to a boil, stirring often. Reduce heat. Simmer, uncovered, for about 1½ hours until thickened. Pour into hot sterilized half-pint (250 mL) jars to within ¼ inch (6 mm) of top. Place sterilized metal lids on jars and screw metal bands on securely. For added assurance against spoilage, process in boiling water bath for 15 minutes. Makes 7 half-pint (250 mL) jars.

2 tbsp. (30 mL): 12 Calories; 0.1 g Total Fat; 162 mg Sodium; trace Protein; 3 g Carbohydrate; 1 g Dietary Fiber

★★★★★★★★★★★★★★★★★★★★★★★★★★★★★★★★★★★★

PICANTE SALSA

The heat in this chunky salsa is adjustable.

Ripe tomatoes, scalded and peeled, stem ends and cores removed	4½ lbs.	2 kg
Whole green chilies (or 1 can of diced, 4 oz., 114 mL, drained)	3	3
Large Spanish onion	1	1
Large green pepper	1	1
Medium red pepper	1	1
Whole jalapeño peppers (or 1 can of diced, 4 oz., 114 mL, drained)	3-6	3-6
Can of tomato paste	5½ oz.	156 mL
White vinegar	¾ cup	175 mL
Brown sugar, packed	¼ cup	60 mL
Coarse (pickling) salt	1 tbsp.	15 mL
Paprika	2 tsp.	10 mL
Garlic powder (or 2 cloves, minced)	½ tsp.	2 mL

Chop first 6 ingredients and place in large pot.

Add remaining 6 ingredients. Heat on medium, uncovered, stirring occasionally, until boiling. Reduce heat. Simmer, stirring occasionally, for 60 minutes until thickened to desired consistency. Near end of cooking, taste for more jalapeño peppers. Add as desired. Fill hot sterilized pint (500 mL) jars to within ½ inch (12 mm) of top. Place sterilized metal lids on jars and screw metal bands on securely. For added assurance against spoilage, process in boiling water bath for 15 minutes. Makes 5 pint (500 mL) jars.

2 tbsp. (30 mL): 11 Calories; 0.1 g Total Fat; 85 mg Sodium; trace Protein; 2 g Carbohydrate; trace Dietary Fiber

SIMPLE PICANTE SALSA

For a mild, chunky salsa, simply omit the crushed red chilies. For hot salsa, add more. Easy to double.

Can of diced tomatoes, with juice (see Note)	28 oz.	796 mL
Can of tomato sauce	7½ oz.	213 mL
Garlic clove, minced	1	1
Small green pepper, chopped	1	1
Small red pepper, chopped	1	1
Dried whole oregano	½ tsp.	2 mL
Coarse (pickling) salt	½ tsp.	2 mL
Dried crushed chilies	½ tsp.	2 mL

Combine all 8 ingredients in large saucepan. Bring to a boil on medium. Boil gently for about 20 minutes, stirring occasionally, until thickened. Cool. Pour into freezer containers to within 1 inch (2.5 cm) of top. Cover with tight-fitting lid. Freeze. Makes 3 cups (750 mL).

2 tbsp. (30 mL): 9 Calories; 0.1 g Total Fat; 141 mg Sodium; trace Protein; 2 g Carbohydrate; trace Dietary Fiber

Note: Use 2¼ pounds (1 kg) fresh tomatoes, stem ends and cores removed; peeled, chopped and cooked.

SASSY SALSA

A bit of a nip. Easy to make hotter or cooler by adjusting the amount of crushed chilies.

Ripe tomatoes, stem ends and cores removed, peeled and chopped	4½ lbs.	2 kg
Medium onions, chopped	3	3
White vinegar	¼ cup	60 mL
Dried crushed chilies	1 tsp.	5 mL
Salt	1½ tsp.	7 mL
Pepper	¼ tsp.	1 mL
Cans of diced green chilies (4 oz., 114 mL, each), with liquid	2	2
Granulated sugar	1 tsp.	5 mL
Paprika	1½ tsp.	7 mL

Combine all 9 ingredients in large pot or Dutch oven. Bring to a boil on medium-high, stirring often. Reduce heat. Simmer for about 1½ hours until thickened. Fill hot sterilized pint (500 mL) jars to within ½ inch (12 mm) of top. Place sterilized metal lids on jars and screw metal bands on securely. For added assurance against spoilage, process in boiling water bath for 15 minutes. May also be frozen. Leave 1 inch (2.5 cm) head space. Makes 3 pint (500 mL) jars.

2 tbsp. (30 mL): 11 Calories; 0.2 g Total Fat; 102 mg Sodium; trace Protein; 3 g Carbohydrate; 1 g Dietary Fiber

BLACK BEAN SALSA

Make a day ahead to allow flavors to blend. Use in Barbecued Fajitas, page 84.

Can of black beans, with liquid	14 oz.	398 mL
Salt	¼ tsp.	1 mL
Cayenne pepper	¼ tsp.	1 mL
Garlic clove, minced	1	1
Lime juice	1 tsp.	5 mL
Chili powder	½ tsp.	2 mL
Finely chopped red onion	½ cup	125 mL
Roasted medium red pepper, peeled and cut into slivers	1	1
Finely chopped fresh cilantro	1 tbsp.	15 mL
Medium tomato, seeded and diced	1	1
Pitted ripe olives, sliced	10	10

Combine first 6 ingredients in medium saucepan. Simmer for 15 minutes, stirring often to prevent scorching, until some of the liquid is evaporated and beans are soft. Remove from heat.

Add remaining 5 ingredients. Stir well. Chill. Makes 2 cups (500 mL).

2 tbsp. (30 mL): 33 Calories; trace Total Fat; 1 mg Sodium; 2 g Protein; 6 g Carbohydrate; trace Dietary Fiber

Keep a large bowl of ice nearby when cutting a lot of onions to draw away the fumes and prevent tears.

★★★★★★★★★★★★★★★★★★★★★★★★★★★

Mexican

WINTER CHILI SAUCE

A good chili sauce to make when you don't have ripe tomatoes, or simply when it is more convenient.

Can of diced tomatoes, with juice (see Note)	28 oz.	796 mL
Large tart apples (such as Granny Smith), peeled, cored and finely chopped	3	3
Large onions, finely chopped	2	2
Finely chopped celery	1 cup	250 mL
Medium red pepper, finely chopped	1	1
Salt	1 ½ tsp.	7 mL
Brown sugar, packed	1 cup	250 mL
Ground cinnamon	½ tsp.	2 mL
Ground cloves	¼ tsp.	1 mL
White vinegar	¾ cup	175 mL

Place first 6 ingredients in large saucepan. Bring to a boil on medium. Reduce heat. Simmer, uncovered, for about 1¼ hours, stirring occasionally, until tender.

Add remaining 4 ingredients. Stir. Return to a boil. Pour into hot sterilized half-pint (250 mL) jars to within ¼ inch (6 mm) of top. Place sterilized metal lids on jars and screw metal bands on securely. For added assurance against spoilage, process in boiling water bath for 15 minutes. Makes 7 half-pint (250 mL) jars.

2 tbsp. (30 mL): 22 Calories; 0.1 g Total Fat; 84 mg Sodium; trace Protein; 6 g Carbohydrate; trace Dietary Fiber

Note: Use 2¼ pounds (1 kg) fresh tomatoes, stem ends and cores removed; peeled, chopped and cooked.

CHILI SAUCE

If too many tomatoes are ripening too fast, consider this as a solution.

Ripe medium tomatoes, peeled, stem ends and cores removed, diced	12	12
Large onions, finely chopped	4	4
Finely chopped celery	1 cup	250 mL
White vinegar	2 cups	500 mL
Brown sugar, packed	2 cups	500 mL
Ground cinnamon	1 tbsp.	15 mL
Ground cloves	1 tsp.	5 mL
Salt	1 tbsp.	15 mL

Combine all 8 ingredients in large saucepan. Heat and stir on medium until boiling. Reduce heat. Simmer, uncovered, for about 1½ hours, stirring occasionally, until thickened. Pour into hot sterilized pint (500 mL) jars to within ½ inch (12 mm) of top. Place sterilized metal lids on jars and screw metal bands on securely. For added assurance against spoilage, process in boiling water bath for 15 minutes. Makes 4 pint (500 mL) jars.

2 tbsp. (30 mL): 31 Calories; 0.1 g Total Fat; 97 mg Sodium; trace Protein; 8 g Carbohydrate; trace Dietary Fiber

When baking always use baking soda from the box in the cupboard, not from the box sitting in your refrigerator. The odors the baking soda has absorbed may result in your baking having an undesirable taste.

SWEET GRILLED SALSA

Serve this warm or cold—great flavor either way. Makes a colorful presentation with grilled fish, chicken, beef or pork.

Medium cobs of corn, husked	3	3
Boiling water, to cover		
Maple (or maple-flavored) syrup	⅓ cup	75 mL
Dried crushed chilies	¼ tsp.	1 mL
Large red onion, cut into ½ inch (12 mm) thick rings	1	1
Medium roma (plum) tomatoes, halved lengthwise and seeded	3	3
Medium zucchini, with peel, cut lengthwise into ¼ inch (6 mm) thick slices	1	1
Finely chopped fresh oregano leaves (or ½ tsp., 2 mL, dried)	2 tsp.	10 mL
Finely chopped fresh sweet basil (or ½ tsp., 2 mL, dried)	2 tsp.	10 mL
Salt	½ tsp.	2 mL
Pepper	¼ tsp.	1 mL
Balsamic vinegar	1-2 tbsp.	15-30 mL

Preheat lightly sprayed electric grill to medium-high. Cook corn in boiling water in large uncovered pot or Dutch oven for 4 minutes.

Combine maple syrup and chilies in small bowl. Drain cobs. Place on grill. Baste with syrup mixture. Cook for about 8 minutes, turning frequently, until golden and slightly charred. Cut kernels from cobs into medium bowl.

Place onion, tomato and zucchini on greased grill. Baste with syrup mixture. Cook for 3 to 5 minutes, turning frequently, until soft and caramelized. Dice. Add to corn kernels.

Season and toss with remaining 4 ingredients. Makes 4 cups (1 L).

2 tbsp. (30 mL): 21 Calories; 0.2 g Total Fat; 44 mg Sodium; trace Protein; 5 g Carbohydrate; 1 g Dietary Fiber

PINEAPPLE SALSA

Great with steak or ham.

Can of pineapple tidbits, drained	8 oz.	227 mL
Chopped red onion	½ cup	125 mL
Chopped fresh cilantro (or parsley)	2 tbsp.	30 mL
Lime juice	1 tbsp.	15 mL
Cayenne pepper	½ tsp.	2 mL

Combine all 5 ingredients in small bowl. Cover. Chill for at least 1 hour to blend flavors. Makes about 1 cup (250 mL).

2 tbsp. (30 mL): 13 Calories; trace Total Fat; 1 mg Sodium; trace Protein; 3 g Carbohydrate; trace Dietary Fiber

TOMATO SALSA

An fresh, easy dip.

Medium tomatoes, diced	2	2
Dried sweet basil	¼ tsp.	1 mL
Dried whole oregano	¼ tsp.	1 mL
Garlic powder	⅛ tsp.	0.5 mL
Salt	¼ tsp.	1 mL
Pepper	¹⁄₁₆ tsp.	0.5 mL
Cooking oil	1 tsp.	5 mL

Combine all 7 ingredients in small bowl. Makes about 1 cup (250 mL).

2 tbsp. (30 mL): 12 Calories; 0.7 g Total Fat; 84 mg Sodium; trace Protein; 1 g Carbohydrate; trace Dietary Fiber

Pictured on page 36.

★★★★★★★★★★★★★★★★★★★★★★★★★★★★★★★★

Brunch & Lunch

W hether you're feeding yourself or a group, there's plenty of choices to liven up a late breakfast or lunch. The crowd will clamor for Fast Fixin' Nacho Casserole, page 48, with soft, warm Chili Biscuits, page 49. What could be simpler than Skillet Chili 'N' Pasta, page 52, or yummy Nacho Pizza, page 57. A Mexican brunch or lunch is a great break from everyday fare!

EGG FAJITAS

Assemble and serve, or have everyone roll their own.

Large onion, halved lengthwise and thinly sliced	1	1
Medium green pepper, slivered	1	1
Medium yellow pepper, slivered	1	1
Water	⅓ cup	75 mL
Can of beans in tomato sauce (or refried beans)	14 oz.	398 mL
Large eggs	9	9
Water	3 tbsp.	50 mL
Chili powder	¼ tsp.	1 mL
Cayenne pepper	⅛ tsp.	0.5 mL
Salt, sprinkle		
Pepper, sprinkle		
Grated Monterey Jack cheese	1½ cups	375 mL
Shredded lettuce, lightly packed	1½ cups	375 mL
Medium tomatoes, diced	2	2
Salsa	⅓ cup	75 mL
Flour tortillas (9 inch, 22 cm, size),warmed, see Tip, page 85	6	6

Simmer onion and peppers in water in large saucepan until soft. Keep warm. Add a bit more water, if necessary, to keep from burning.

Heat beans in small saucepan until hot.

Combine next 6 ingredients in medium bowl. Beat lightly. Pour into greased heated frying pan. Heat and stir until eggs are set.

Spoon egg mixture, beans, onion mixture, cheese, lettuce, tomato and salsa onto tortillas. Roll up, folding in 1 end. Makes 6 fajitas.

1 fajita: 433 Calories; 17.7 g Total Fat; 896 mg Sodium; 25 g Protein; 56 g Carbohydrate; 8 g Dietary Fiber

EGG ENCHILADAS

A very different breakfast. Tortillas, corn and eggs go well together.

FILLING

Margarine (or butter)	1 tsp.	5 mL
Chopped onion	¼ cup	60 mL
Large hard-boiled eggs, chopped	8	8
Can of diced green chilies, drained	4 oz.	114 mL
Grated Monterey Jack cheese	½ cup	125 mL
Grated Parmesan cheese	2 tbsp.	30 mL
Salt	¼ tsp.	1 mL
Corn tortillas (6 inch, 15 cm, size), see Note	12	12

SAUCE

Can of cream-style corn	14 oz.	398 mL
Seeded and diced tomato (about 2 small)	¾ cup	175 mL
Prepared mustard	1 tsp.	5 mL
Granulated sugar	½ tsp.	2 mL
Onion powder	½ tsp.	2 mL
Garlic powder	½ tsp.	2 mL
Grated Monterey Jack cheese	½ cup	125 mL
Sour cream, for garnish (optional)	½ cup	125 mL
Chopped chives, for garnish (optional)	2 tsp.	10 mL

Filling: Melt margarine in saucepan. Add onion. Sauté until soft. Remove from heat.

Stir in next 5 ingredients.

Spoon ¼ cup (60 mL) egg mixture down center of each tortilla. Roll snugly. Place, seam side down, in pan large enough to hold single layer. Cover pan with damp cloth while rolling remainder to prevent cracking.

Sauce: Stir first 6 ingredients together in bowl. Pour over enchiladas.

Sprinkle with cheese. Bake, uncovered, in 350°F (175°C) oven for about 25 minutes until bubbly hot.

Spoon sour cream across enchiladas. Top with chives. Makes 12.

1 enchilada: 218 Calories; 8.8 g Total Fat; 351 mg Sodium; 11 g Protein; 26 g Carbohydrate; 2 g Dietary Fiber

Note: To prevent tortillas from cracking, cover with damp cloth and warm slightly in microwave before filling and rolling.

BREAKFAST BURRITO

A mild burrito dipped in a zesty sauce. Serve with salsa for dipping.

Bacon slice, diced	1	1
Finely chopped onion	1 tsp.	5 mL
Large egg, fork-beaten	1	1
Diced cooked chicken	¼ cup	60 mL
Salt, sprinkle		
Pepper, sprinkle		
Flour tortillas (7 inch, 18 cm, size)	2	2
Grated medium Cheddar cheese	2 tbsp.	30 mL

Sauté bacon and onion in frying pan until onion is soft.

Add egg, chicken, salt and pepper. Scramble-fry until egg is set.

Heat tortillas on medium in another frying pan. Lay on plate. Put half of cheese down center of each. Divide filling between them. Roll. Serves 1.

1 serving: 540 Calories; 25.2 g Total Fat; 618 mg Sodium; 31 g Protein; 45 g Carbohydrate; trace Dietary Fiber

★★★★★★★★★★★★★★★★★★★★★★★★★★★★★★★★

OVEN BURRITOS

Several breakfast ingredients, spiced and rolled in tortillas.

Bacon slices, cut into ½ inch (12 mm) pieces	8	8
Cooking oil	2 tsp.	10 mL
Sliced fresh mushrooms	1 cup	250 mL
Finely chopped green pepper	½ cup	125 mL
Chopped onion	½ cup	125 mL
Large eggs	8	8
Water (or milk)	3 tbsp.	50 mL
Grated Monterey Jack cheese	¼ cup	60 mL
Salsa	3 tbsp.	50 mL
Chopped chives	1 tbsp.	15 mL
Garlic powder	¼ tsp.	1 mL
Flour tortillas (9 inch, 22 cm, size)	4	4
Grated medium Cheddar cheese	2 tbsp.	30 mL
Grated Monterey Jack cheese	2 tbsp.	30 mL
Sour cream (optional)		
Salsa (optional)		

Cook bacon in frying pan until almost crisp. Drain. Remove bacon to paper towel.

Heat cooking oil in same frying pan. Add mushrooms, green pepper and onion. Sauté until soft. Add bacon. Keep warm.

Beat eggs together in medium bowl. Add water, first amounts of Monterey Jack cheese and salsa, chives and garlic powder. Beat to mix. Pour into non-stick frying pan sprayed with no-stick cooking spray. Heat on medium-low, stirring often, until eggs are partially set. Add mushroom mixture. Cover. Heat until set. Cut into pieces to fill tortillas.

Divide mixture and place down center of each tortilla. Roll. Arrange, seam side down, in single layer in greased 9 x 9 inch (22 x 22 cm) baking dish.

Sprinkle with Cheddar cheese and second amount of Monterey Jack cheese. Bake in 350°F (175°C) oven for 20 to 30 minutes until heated through.

Serve with sour cream and salsa. Serves 4.

1 serving: 445 Calories; 24 g Total Fat; 631 mg Sodium; 25 g Protein; 31 g Carbohydrate; 1 g Dietary Fiber

---

To convert Fahrenheit into Centigrade, subtract 32, multiply by 5, then divide by 9. To convert Centigrade into Fahrenheit, multiply by 9, divide by 5 and add 32. Or just refer to our handy chart on p. 119.

CHICKEN BURRITOS

Serve these wonderful burritos with sour cream for dipping.

Cooking oil	2 tbsp.	30 mL
Boneless, skinless chicken breasts, cut into strips	2	2
Medium green pepper, chopped	1	1
Medium red pepper, chopped	1	1
Green onions, sliced	4	4
Finely chopped canned jalapeño pepper	1 tbsp.	15 mL
Ground coriander	1 tbsp.	15 mL
Garlic powder (or 1 clove, minced)	¼ tsp.	1 mL
Flour tortillas (10 inch, 25 cm, size)	8	8
Medium tomatoes, seeded and diced	2	2
Grated medium Cheddar cheese	1 cup	250 mL
Grated medium Cheddar cheese	¾ cup	175 mL

Heat cooking oil in frying pan. Add next 7 ingredients. Stir-fry until chicken is no longer pink and peppers are soft.

Spoon ⅛ of chicken mixture in a row off center on each tortilla. Divide tomato and first amount of cheese evenly on top of chicken mixture. Roll tortillas as for jelly roll, tucking in sides. Arrange, seam side down, in single layer in 9 x 13 inch (22 x 33 cm) pan.

Sprinkle with second amount of cheese. Cover. Heat in 350°F (175°C) oven for 25 to 40 minutes to heat through. Serves 4.

1 serving: 691 Calories; 26.8 g Total Fat; 805 mg Sodium; 39 g Protein; 72 g Carbohydrate; 2 g Dietary Fiber

Pictured on front cover.

BURRITOS

These are flavorful on their own but with salsa and sour cream they are extra good and spiced just right.

Cooking oil	2 tsp.	10 mL
Chopped onion	1¼ cups	300 mL
Garlic cloves, minced (or ½ tsp., 2 mL, garlic powder)	2	2
Medium potatoes, quartered	2	2
Boiling water, to cover		
Can of kidney (or pinto) beans, drained and rinsed	14 oz.	398 mL
Dried whole oregano	½ tsp.	2 mL
Ground cumin	½ tsp.	2 mL
Salt	½ tsp.	2 mL
Pepper	⅛ tsp.	0.5 mL
Flour tortillas (8 inch, 20 cm, size)	6	6
Salsa (optional)		
Sour cream (optional)		

Heat cooking oil in frying pan. Add onion and garlic. Sauté until soft and golden. Remove from heat.

Cook potatoes in boiling water until tender-crisp. Cool enough to handle. Dice. Add to onion mixture.

Empty kidney beans into shallow pan or bowl. Add oregano, cumin, salt and pepper. Mash well with fork. Add to onion mixture. Heat, stirring often, until hot.

Wrap tortillas in foil. Heat in 350°F (175°C) oven for 8 to 10 minutes. Divide bean mixture down center of each tortillas. Fold 1 side over, then ends, then roll. Filling should be completely enclosed. If not serving immediately, wrap in foil and place in 200°F (95°C) oven.

Serve with salsa and sour cream. Makes 6 burritos.

1 burrito: 240 Calories; 2.5 g Total Fat; 632 mg Sodium; 9 g Protein; 46 g Carbohydrate; 6 g Dietary Fiber

★★★★★★★★★★★★★★★★★★★★★★★★★★★★★★

CREAMY BURRITOS

Taste will vary depending on the strength of the salsa you use.

Cooking oil	1 tbsp.	15 mL
Ground chicken	1 lb.	454 g
Light cream cheese, cut up	8 oz.	250 g
Salsa	1½ cups	375 mL
Frozen chopped spinach, thawed and squeezed dry	10 oz.	300 g
Whole wheat flour tortillas (10 inch, 25 cm, size)	6	6
Salsa	1½ cups	375 mL
Grated medium Cheddar cheese	½ cup	125 mL

Heat cooking oil in frying pan. Add ground chicken. Scramble-fry until no longer pink.

Add cream cheese, first amount of salsa and spinach. Heat and stir until hot. Makes 4 cups (1 L) filling.

Place about ⅔ cup (150 mL) filling on each tortilla. Roll up, folding in ends to completely enclose filling. Arrange burritos, seam side down, in single layer in greased 9 x 13 inch (22 x 33 cm) baking dish.

Spoon second amount of salsa down length of each burrito. Sprinkle with cheese. Bake in 350°F (175°C) oven for about 25 minutes. Makes 6 burritos.

1 burrito: 458 Calories; 15.3 g Total Fat; 1454 mg Sodium; 33 g Protein; 48 g Carbohydrate; 4 g Dietary Fiber

TACO ON A PLATTER

The less messy way to eat tacos.

Lean ground beef	2 lbs.	900 g
Medium onion, chopped	1	1
Can of tomato paste	14 oz.	398 mL
Can of crushed tomatoes	14 oz.	398 mL
Chili powder	2 tbsp.	30 mL
Ground cumin	1 tsp.	5 mL
Garlic powder	½ tsp.	2 mL
Salt	2 tsp.	10 mL
Can of beans in tomato sauce	28 oz.	796 mL
Broken corn chips	2 cups	500 mL
Hot cooked long grain white rice	2 cups	500 mL
Grated medium Cheddar cheese	2 cups	500 mL
Medium red onion, chopped	1	1
Head of iceberg lettuce, shredded	1	1
Medium tomatoes, chopped	3	3
Sliced pitted ripe olives	⅓ cup	75 mL

Scramble-fry ground beef and onion in large non-stick frying pan until beef is no longer pink and onion is soft. Drain.

Add next 6 ingredients. Mix well. Simmer, uncovered, for 15 minutes.

Add beans. Heat through.

Layer corn chips, rice, beef mixture, cheese, red onion, lettuce, tomato and olives on large platter. Serves 12.

1 serving: 429 Calories; 17.7 g Total Fat; 1032 mg Sodium; 26 g Protein; 44 g Carbohydrate; 10 g Dietary Fiber

To Make Ahead: Make the beef sauce the day before. Cover and chill. Heat thoroughly just before assembling.

Taco Cheese Burgers

The hamburger for the Mexican food lover.

Lean ground beef	1 lb.	454 g
Dry bread crumbs	¼ cup	60 mL
Large egg, fork-beaten	1	1
Small onion, finely chopped	1	1
Chili powder	1 tbsp.	15 mL
Dry mustard	½ tsp.	2 mL
Salt	½ tsp.	2 mL
Freshly ground pepper, to taste		
Thin slices Monterey Jack cheese	4	4
Hamburger buns, split	4	4
Salsa (optional)		
Sour cream (optional)		

Combine first 8 ingredients in medium bowl. Mix well. Shape into 8 thin patties.

Place cheese slices on 4 patties. Top with remaining 4 patties. Pinch edges to seal. Barbecue patties on medium-high for 6 to 8 minutes per side until no longer pink.

Place buns, cut side down, on grill until lightly toasted.

Serve with salsa or sour cream. Makes 4 burgers.

1 burger (with bun): 440 Calories; 20 g Total Fat; 803 mg Sodium; 32 g Protein; 32 g Carbohydrate; 2 g Dietary Fiber

To Make Ahead: Make and freeze single patties. Fully defrost before adding cheese and doubling up.

Fast Fixin' Nacho Casserole

Quick way to use leftover beef. Only 5 minutes to prepare.

Coarsely chopped cooked lean beef	1¼ cups	300 mL
Salsa	¾ cup	175 mL
Grated Monterey Jack cheese	⅓ cup	75 mL
Grated Monterey Jack cheese	⅔ cup	150 mL

Combine beef, salsa and first amount of cheese in medium bowl. Lightly spray 1 quart (1 L) casserole with no-stick cooking spray. Turn beef mixture into casserole. Cover. Bake in 350°F (175°C) oven for 20 minutes.

Top with second amount of cheese. Bake, uncovered, in 350°F (175°C) oven for 10 minutes until cheese is melted. Serves 4.

1 serving: 269 Calories; 14.8 g Total Fat; 216 mg Sodium; 21 g Protein; 13 g Carbohydrate; 1 g Dietary Fiber

To deter insects from the dried beans you're storing, put a few dried chilies in the jar with the beans. Secure the lid tightly.

CHILI BISCUITS

Burnt orange color to these surprising biscuits.

All-purpose flour	2 cups	500 mL
Baking powder	1 tbsp.	15 mL
Salt	¾ tsp.	4 mL
Chili powder	1 tsp.	5 mL
Onion powder	1½ tsp.	7 mL
Hard margarine (or butter)	¼ cup	60 mL
Grated sharp Cheddar cheese	1 cup	250 mL
Tomato juice	¾ cup	175 mL

Combine first 5 ingredients in small bowl. Cut in margarine until crumbly.

Stir in cheese and tomato juice until dough forms a soft ball. Turn out onto lightly floured surface. Knead 8 to 10 times. Pat or roll ¾ inch (2 cm) thick. Cut into 2 inch (5 cm) rounds. Arrange on greased baking sheet. Bake in 425°F (220°C) oven for about 12 minutes until browned. Serve warm. Makes 16 biscuits.

1 biscuit: 122 Calories; 5.7 g Total Fat; 252 mg Sodium; 4 g Protein; 14 g Carbohydrate; 1 g Dietary Fiber

TACO CORNMEAL BREAD

An orange shade to this yummy loaf. Perfect to eat with chili or even just with margarine.

Granulated sugar	2 tsp.	10 mL
Warm water	½ cup	125 mL
Envelopes of active dry yeast (¼ oz., 8 g, each)	2	2
Milk	1½ cups	375 mL
Large eggs	2	2
Liquid honey	½ cup	125 mL
Cooking oil	½ cup	125 mL
Salt	2 tsp.	10 mL
Envelopes of taco seasoning mix (1¼ oz., 35 g, each)	2	2
Whole wheat flour	2 cups	500 mL
Cornmeal	1½ cups	375 mL
Whole wheat flour	1 cup	250 mL
All-purpose flour, approximately	3¾ cups	925 mL
Milk, for brushing tops	2 tsp.	10 mL

Stir sugar into warm water in small bowl. Sprinkle yeast over top. Let stand for 10 minutes. Stir to dissolve yeast.

Heat milk in small saucepan until lukewarm.

Beat eggs in large bowl. Add milk and yeast mixture. Add next 6 ingredients. Beat on low to moisten. Beat on high until smooth.

Work in second amount of whole wheat flour. Work in enough all-purpose flour until dough pulls away from sides of bowl. Turn out onto lightly floured surface. Knead 8 to 10 times until smooth and elastic. Place in greased bowl, turning once to grease top. Cover with tea towel. Let stand in oven with light on and door closed for 1½ to 1¾ hours until doubled in bulk. Punch dough down. Divide into 2 equal portions. Shape into loaves. Place in 2 greased 9 x 5 x 3 inch (22 x 12.5 x 7.5 cm) loaf pans. Cover with tea towel. Let stand in oven with light on and door closed for about 45 minutes until doubled in size.

Brush tops with milk. Bake in 375°F (190°C) oven for about 30 minutes. Turn out onto racks to cool. Makes 2 loaves, for a total of 20 slices.

1 slice: 302 Calories; 7.5 g Total Fat; 736 mg Sodium; 8 g Protein; 52 g Carbohydrate; 4 g Dietary Fiber

Pictured on page 54.

CHIMICHANGAS

These deep-fried burritos make a good hot lunch with a nice crisp salad.

Cooking oil	2 tbsp.	30 mL
Beef stew meat, cubed	1 lb.	454 g
Boiling water	1 cup	250 mL
Beef bouillon cubes (⅕ oz., 6 g, each)	2	2
Medium onion, chopped	1	1
Margarine (or butter)	2 tbsp.	30 mL
Salt	1 tsp.	5 mL
Garlic powder (or 1 clove, minced)	¼ tsp.	1 mL
Medium tomato, cut up	1	1
Can of diced green chilies, drained	4 oz.	114 mL
Flour tortillas (10 inch, 25 cm, size)	6	6
Cooking oil, for deep-frying		
Grated medium Cheddar (or Monterey Jack) cheese	¾ cup	175 mL
Salsa, warmed	¾ cup	175 mL

Heat first amount of cooking oil in roaster. Add stew meat. Brown well on medium until no longer pink. Stir in water and bouillon cubes until dissolved.

Process next 6 ingredients in blender. Pour over beef. Stir. Cover. Bake in 300°F (150°C) oven for 2 hours until beef is very tender. If pieces are large, shred with fork. If there is a lot of sauce, bring to a boil on stovetop, uncovered, until mostly evaporated.

Spoon ⅙ of beef mixture along side of tortilla. Turn side over, fold ends in and roll up. Pin with toothpick to keep filling in. Deep-fry in hot 375°F (190°C) cooking oil, turning to brown both sides. Remove with slotted spoon to paper towel to drain.

Sprinkle with cheese. Spoon salsa on top. Serves 6.

1 serving: 505 Calories; 25.3 g Total Fat; 1779 mg Sodium; 27 g Protein; 42 g Carbohydrate; 2 g Dietary Fiber

GRILLED QUESADILLAS

Easy, fast and delicious with only a few ingredients.

Grated Monterey Jack cheese	½ cup	125 mL
Flour tortillas (10 inch, 25 cm, size)	2	2
Salsa	¼ cup	60 mL
Chopped green onion	2 tsp.	10 mL
Finely diced red pepper	1 tbsp.	15 mL

Preheat lightly sprayed electric grill for 5 minutes to high. Sprinkle ½ of cheese over 1 tortilla. Drizzle salsa over cheese.

Sprinkle with green onion and red pepper. Sprinkle with remaining cheese. Cover with second tortilla. Place on grill. Heat, uncovered, for 2 minutes. Carefully turn over. Heat for 2 to 3 minutes until cheese is melted and tortillas are crispy and browned. Cuts into 4 wedges each, for a total of 8 wedges.

1 wedge: 74 Calories; 2.5 g Total Fat; 214 mg Sodium; 3 g Protein; 9 g Carbohydrate; trace Dietary Fiber

To cut an avocado easily, slice lengthwise around the fruit, then twist the two halves to separate from the pit. If needed, you can pry the pit out with the tip of a teaspoon.

QUESADILLAS

Bake these kay-sah-DEE-yahs in the oven. Everybody's favorite. Serve with guacamole, salsa and sour cream.

Cream cheese, softened	4 oz.	125 g
Salsa	⅓ cup	75 mL
Chopped green pepper	⅓ cup	75 mL
Large tomato, seeded and diced	1	1
Can of diced green chilies, drained	4 oz.	114 mL
Green onions, chopped	3	3
Flour tortillas (10 inch, 25 cm, size)	6	6
Grated Monterey Jack (or medium Cheddar) cheese	1½ cups	375 mL

Mash cream cheese and salsa together with fork in shallow bowl or plate. Set aside.

Toss next 4 ingredients in small bowl.

Spread ½ of each tortilla with cream cheese mixture to ½ inch (12 mm) from edge. Sprinkle green pepper mixture over cream cheese mixture.

Sprinkle each tortilla with grated cheese. Fold uncovered half over filling. Press edges lightly with hand. Arrange on ungreased baking sheet. Bake in 425°F (220°C) oven for 10 to 15 minutes or toast under broiler. Cut into 4 wedges each, for a total of 24 wedges.

1 wedge: 94 Calories; 4.3 g Total Fat; 128 mg Sodium; 4 g Protein; 10 g Carbohydrate; trace Dietary Fiber

QUESADILLA APPETIZERS: Use about 10 flour tortillas (8 inch, 20 cm, size). Follow above recipe. Cut each into 6 wedges, for a total of 60 wedges.

FAJITA SANDWICHES

Serve with fresh fruit for a simple weeknight meal.

Lean ground chicken (or turkey)	1 lb.	454 g
Garlic cloves, minced	2	2
Lime juice	1 tbsp.	15 mL
Dried crushed chilies	¼ tsp.	1 mL
Low-sodium soy sauce	2 tsp.	10 mL
Paprika	¼ tsp.	1 mL
Salt	½ tsp.	2 mL
Medium onion, sliced into ½ inch (12 mm) slices	1	1
Medium red pepper, cut into thin slivers	1	1
Medium yellow pepper, cut into thin slivers	1	1
Lime juice	1 tbsp.	15 mL
Low-sodium soy sauce	1 tbsp.	15 mL
Granulated sugar	1 tsp.	5 mL
Ground coriander	¼ tsp.	1 mL
Freshly ground pepper	¼ tsp.	1 mL
Salsa	½ cup	125 mL
Crusty buns	6	6

Lightly grease non-stick frying pan or wok. Sauté chicken with garlic for 3 to 4 minutes. Add first amount of lime juice, chilies, soy sauce, paprika and salt. Sauté for 4 to 5 minutes until chicken is no longer pink.

Add onion, peppers, second amount of lime juice, soy sauce, sugar, coriander and pepper. Stir-fry for 4 to 5 minutes until vegetables are tender. Add salsa. Stir until hot. Remove from heat.

Cut buns in half. Remove just a bit of soft center from each bun. Fill 6 halves with ¾ to 1 cup (175 to 250 mL) fajita mixture and top with other bun half. Makes 6 sandwiches.

1 sandwich: 279 Calories; 3.8 g Total Fat; 1097 mg Sodium; 22 g Protein; 39 g Carbohydrate; 2 g Dietary Fiber

CHILIES RELLENOS CASSEROLE

Never was a casserole so easy. Cheddar cheese rather than the usual Monterey Jack gives a superb flavor. Serve hot as a side dish or cold as an appetizer.

Can of diced green chilies, with liquid	4 oz.	114 mL
Medium Cheddar cheese	½ lb.	225 g
Large eggs	2	2
Milk	2 cups	500 mL
All-purpose flour	½ cup	125 mL
Salt	1 tsp.	5 mL
Pepper	⅛ tsp.	0.5 mL

Spread diced chilies with liquid in 8 x 8 inch (20 x 20 cm) baking dish or shallow casserole. Slice cheese. Layer on top.

Process remaining 5 ingredients in blender until smooth. Pour over chilies. Bake, uncovered, in 350°F (175°C) oven for 45 to 50 minutes until knife inserted in center comes out clean. Serves 6.

1 serving: 257 Calories; 15.1 g Total Fat; 972 mg Sodium; 16 g Protein; 14 g Carbohydrate; 1 g Dietary Fiber

SKILLET CHILI 'N' PASTA

Only a skillet (frying pan) and 15 minutes are needed to prepare this easy one-dish meal.

Lean ground beef	¾ lb.	340 g
Medium onion, diced	1	1
Garlic clove, minced	1	1
Can of stewed tomatoes, with juice, chopped	28 oz.	796 mL
Tomato juice	1 cup	250 mL
Can of kidney beans, with liquid	14 oz.	398 mL
Chili powder	1 tbsp.	15 mL
Fusilli pasta, uncooked	1 cup	250 mL
Chopped fresh sweet basil	2 tbsp.	30 mL

Scramble-fry ground beef, onion and garlic in non-stick frying pan until beef is no longer pink and onion is soft. Drain.

Add next 4 ingredients. Bring to a boil.

Add pasta and basil. Bring to a boil. Cover. Simmer for 15 minutes until pasta is tender. Serves 4.

1 serving: 383 Calories; 8.4 g Total Fat; 1198 mg Sodium; 27 g Protein; 53 g Carbohydrate; 11 g Dietary Fiber

1. Corny Beef Enchiladas, page 99
2. Steak Fajitas, page 86
3. Spinach Salad, page 63

TACOS

A great do-it-yourself meal. Just fill your taco shell with layers.

Can of refried beans	14 oz.	398 mL
Taco shells	10	10
Salsa	¼ cup	60 mL
Chopped head lettuce	1 cup	250 mL
Medium tomato, diced	1	1
Small red (or other mild) onion, cut into slivers (optional)	1	1
Grated medium Cheddar (or Monterey Jack) cheese	½ cup	125 mL
Sour cream (optional)	6 tbsp.	100 mL

Heat beans in small saucepan. Divide among taco shells.

Divide remaining 6 ingredients in layers among taco shells. Makes 10 tacos.

1 taco: 125 Calories; 4.5 g Total Fat; 255 mg Sodium; 5 g Protein; 17 g Carbohydrate; 3 g Dietary Fiber

TRENDY TACOS

A good do-it-yourself meal.

Lean ground chicken	1 lb.	454 g
Cooking oil	1 tbsp.	15 mL
Chili powder	1½ tsp.	7 mL
Salt	½ tsp.	2 mL
Pepper	⅛ tsp.	0.5 mL
Dried whole oregano	¼ tsp.	1 mL
Garlic powder	¼ tsp.	1 mL
Paprika	1 tsp.	5 mL
Taco shells	10	10
Medium tomatoes, diced	2	2
Shredded lettuce	1½ cups	375 mL
Onion slivers (optional)	⅓ cup	75 mL
Grated medium or sharp Cheddar cheese	¾ cup	175 mL
Pitted ripe olives, sliced (optional)	10	10
Sour cream	⅔ cup	150 mL

Scramble-fry chicken in cooking oil in frying pan until no longer pink.

Add next 6 ingredients. Mix.

Spoon about 2 tbsp. (30 mL) chicken mixture into each taco shell. Divide remaining 6 ingredients in layers among taco shells. Makes 10 tacos.

1 taco: 182 Calories; 9.6 g Total Fat; 235 mg Sodium; 15 g Protein; 10 g Carbohydrate; 1 g Dietary Fiber

Pictured on page 36.

1. Taco Cornmeal Bread, page 49
2. Pinto Tortilla Soup, page 65
3. Corn Chili Soup, page 68

Props Courtesy Of: Treasure Barrel

TACOS

A very different taco. Most enjoyable. Do not freeze.

Frozen breaded fish sticks	2	2
Taco shells	2	2
Taco (or seafood) sauce	1 tbsp.	15 mL
Chopped lettuce	¼ cup	60 mL
Tomato slice, diced	1	1
Grated medium Cheddar cheese	2 tbsp.	30 mL
Sour cream (optional)	1 tbsp.	15 mL

Heat fish sticks in frying pan or according to package directions.

Put 1 fish stick in each taco shell. Divide remaining 5 ingredients in layers among taco shells. Makes 2 tacos.

1 taco: 172 Calories; 8.2 g Total Fat; 329 mg Sodium; 8 g Protein; 18 g Carbohydrate; 1 g Dietary Fiber

---

To reduce the heat of hot peppers, remove the white veins and seeds before using in recipes.

FLOUR TORTILLAS

Very easy to make. Keep some in the freezer for a snack by themselves, or as a quick lunch with a filling.

All-purpose flour	2 cups	500 mL
Baking powder	1 tsp.	5 mL
Salt	1 tsp.	5 mL
Hard margarine (or butter)	¼ cup	60 mL
Water	⅔ cup	150 mL

Place flour, baking powder and salt in medium bowl. Cut in margarine until crumbly.

Add water. Stir until dough forms a ball. If too dry, add water, 1 tbsp. (15 mL) at a time, until dough firms. Turn out onto lightly floured surface. Knead 6 to 8 times. Cover with inverted bowl. Let rest for 20 minutes. Divide into 10 portions. Roll out, 1 portion at a time, as thin as possible. Invert 7 inch (18 cm) bowl or 8 inch (20 cm) plate onto dough. Cut around edge. Repeat. Place 1 tortilla on medium-hot ungreased frying pan. Some dark spots will appear in 15 to 20 seconds. Turn. Brown 15 to 20 seconds on second side until dark spots appear. Keep warm in tea towel. Cool. Wrap airtight to store. Makes 10 to 12 tortillas.

1 tortilla: 141 Calories; 5.2 g Total Fat; 331 mg Sodium; 3 g Protein; 20 g Carbohydrate; 1 g Dietary Fiber

★★★★★★★★★★★★★★★★★★★★★★★★★★★★★★★★★★

Tex-Mex Pizza

A bit of crunch from the cornmeal crust. Green chilies add a southwestern flavor. A full-meal deal.

CORNMEAL BISCUIT MIX CRUST

Biscuit mix	2 cups	500 mL
Yellow cornmeal	⅓ cup	75 mL
Water	½ cup	125 mL
Can of refried beans	14 oz.	398 mL
Lean ground beef	1 lb.	454 g
Chopped onion	½ cup	125 mL
Can of tomato sauce	7½ oz.	213 mL
Can of diced green chilies, drained	4 oz.	114 mL
Beef bouillon powder	2 tsp.	10 mL
Chili powder	1 tsp.	5 mL
Grated Monterey Jack Cheese	1½ cups	375 mL

Cornmeal Biscuit Mix Crust: Combine all 3 ingredients in medium bowl. Stir until soft ball forms. May need to add 1 tbsp. (15 mL) more water. Dough should be quite sticky. Using greased hands, press into greased 12 inch (30 cm) pizza pan, forming rim around edge. Bake in 425°F (220°C) oven for 5 minutes.

Spread refried beans on crust.

Scramble-fry ground beef and onion in non-stick frying pan until onion is soft and beef is no longer pink. Drain.

Add tomato sauce, green chilies, bouillon powder and chili powder. Stir together. Spread on refried beans.

Sprinkle cheese over top. Bake on bottom rack in 425°F (220°C) oven for 15 to 20 minutes. Cuts into 8 wedges.

1 wedge: 411 Calories; 16.8 g Total Fat; 1134 mg Sodium; 23 g Protein; 42 g Carbohydrate; 4 g Dietary Fiber

Nacho Pizza

Forever popular. Best served hot or warm.

Refrigerator crescent-style rolls (8 per tube)	8 oz.	235 g
Can of jalapeño bean dip (10½ oz., 298 mL)	½	½
Onion salt	⅛ tsp.	0.5 mL
Garlic salt	⅛ tsp.	0.5 mL
Cayenne pepper	⅛ tsp.	0.5 mL
Grated medium Cheddar cheese	1 cup	250 mL
Broken corn chips	⅔ cup	150 mL
Seeded and diced tomato	½ cup	125 mL
Chopped green onion	¼ cup	60 mL
Grated medium Cheddar cheese	1 cup	250 mL

Unroll dough. Press to fit in greased 12 inch (30 cm) pizza pan. Press seams together, forming rim around edge. Bake in 375°F (190°C) oven for about 6 minutes until just turning golden. Cool.

Mash bean dip, onion salt, garlic salt and cayenne pepper together in small bowl. Spread on crust.

Sprinkle with first amount of cheese and corn chips. Scatter tomato, green onion and second amount of cheese over top. Return to oven. Bake for 10 minutes. Cuts into 8 wedges.

1 wedge: 214 Calories; 14.1 g Total Fat; 519 mg Sodium; 10 g Protein; 12 g Carbohydrate; 1 g Dietary Fiber

Pictured on page 72.

RUNCH & LUNCH 57

Salads

Vegetables and dressing are the starting blocks of many salads, but it doesn't have to end there. Ground beef and taco seasoning mix liven up two renditions of Taco Salad, page 60, while Corn Chip Salad, page 62, has an extra crunch. Papaya and pineapple team up in colorful Fruit Salad, page 61, to freshen a hot summer day. And the eye-catching Guacamole Mold, page 62, is great as a salad or a dip.

MEXICAN SALAD

This is a one-dish lunch, where even the salad bowl gets eaten!

Lean ground beef	½ lb.	225 g
Taco seasoning mix	4 tsp.	20 mL
Water	½ cup	125 mL
Can of pinto beans, drained and rinsed	14 oz.	398 mL
Shredded iceberg lettuce	4 cups	1 L
Small red pepper, diced	1	1
Very thinly sliced red onion	1 cup	250 mL
Medium tomato, diced	1	1
Tortilla Bowls, page 59	6	6
CHILI DRESSING		
Non-fat plain yogurt	½ cup	125 mL
Non-fat sour cream	½ cup	125 mL
Chili sauce	3 tbsp.	50 mL
Onion powder	½ tsp.	2 mL
Garlic powder	⅛ tsp.	0.5 mL
Salt	¼ tsp.	1 mL

Scramble-fry ground beef in non-stick frying pan until no longer pink. Drain. Stir in taco seasoning and water. Simmer until all liquid is evaporated. Cool to room temperature.

Combine beans, lettuce, red pepper, red onion and tomato in medium bowl. Toss together. Stir in beef mixture.

Fill tortilla bowls with beef mixture.

Chili Dressing: Combine all 6 ingredients in small bowl. Drizzle over top of beef mixture. Makes 6 cups (9.5 L).

1 cup (250 mL) salad only: 149 Calories; 3.7 g Total Fat; 721 mg Sodium;12 g Protein; 18 g Carbohydrate; 3 g Dietary Fiber

TORTILLA BOWLS

Make as many tortilla bowls as you need. The microwave method is better for corn tortillas—they tend to crack in the oven.

Corn (or flour) tortilla (6 to 7 inch, 15 to 18 cm, size)   1   1

Microwave Oven Method: Lightly grease bottom and outside of 2 cup (500 mL) microwave-safe liquid measure.

1. Turn measure upside down. Press tortilla over bottom and sides. Microwave on high (100%) for 1 minute.
2. Using oven mitts, again press tortilla around measure. Microwave on high (100%) for about 1 minute until brown spots begin to appear. Press tortilla against measure again if necessary.
3. Turn out onto rack to cool.

Conventional Oven Method: Lightly grease bottom and outside of 2 cup (500 mL) oven-safe liquid measure.

1. Turn measure upside down onto baking sheet. Press tortilla over bottom and sides.
2. Bake in 325°F (160°C) oven for 7 to 10 minutes, occasionally pressing tortilla against liquid measure, until brown spots appear.
3. Turn out onto rack to cool.

1 tortilla bowl: 89 Calories; 1.5 g Total Fat; 71 mg Sodium; 3 g Protein; 17 g Carbohydrate; 1 g Dietary Fiber

Note: For larger bowl, use 10 inch (25 cm) flour tortilla over 4 cup (1 L) liquid measure.

Pictured on front cover.

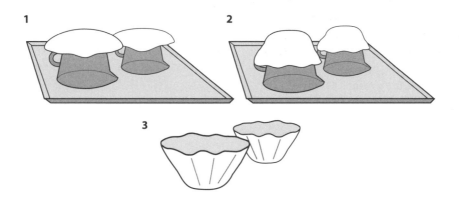

TACO SALAD

*Quick and easy. Make beef mixture ahead. Reheat
and assemble just before serving. Sour cream
makes the perfect garnish. May be served in
Tortilla Bowls, page 49.*

Lean ground beef	1 lb.	454 g
Chopped onion	1 cup	250 mL
Cooking oil	2 tsp.	10 mL
Envelope of taco seasoning mix	1¼ oz.	35 g
Can of diced tomatoes, with juice	14 oz.	398 mL
Grated light sharp Cheddar cheese	1 cup	250 mL
Cut or torn lettuce	6 cups	1.5 L
Medium tomatoes, diced	2	2
Grated light medium or sharp Cheddar cheese	½ cup	125 mL
Green onions, chopped	2	2
Broken tortilla chips	½ cup	125 mL

Scramble-fry ground beef and onion in cooking oil
in large frying pan until onion is soft and is no
longer pink. Drain.

Add seasoning mix, tomatoes with juice and first
amount of cheese. Heat and stir until cheese is
melted.

Divide lettuce among 6 plates. Scatter diced
tomato on each. Spoon hot beef mixture on top.
Sprinkle with second amount of cheese. Scatter
green onion and tortilla chips over top. Serves 6.

1 serving: 304 Calories; 16.5 g Total Fat; 997 mg Sodium;
24 g Protein; 16 g Carbohydrate; 3 g Dietary Fiber

Pictured on front cover.

TACO SALAD

*It's all here—protein, greens, crispiness and good
taste.*

Lean ground chicken	1 lb.	454 g
Cooking oil	1 tbsp.	15 mL
Can of kidney beans, with liquid	14 oz.	398 mL
Envelope of taco seasoning mix	1¼ oz.	35 g
Medium head of lettuce, cut up	1	1
Medium tomato, diced	1	1
Green onions, sliced	3	3
Peeled, sliced cucumber	1 cup	250 mL
Ripe avocado, peeled, pitted and diced	1	1
Pimiento-stuffed green olives, halved	12	12
Grated medium Cheddar cheese	½ cup	125 mL
Bag of plain tortilla chips, crumbled	6 oz.	170 g
Thousand Island dressing	1 cup	250 mL

Scramble-fry ground chicken in cooking oil until no
pink remains.

Stir in kidney beans with liquid and seasoning mix.
Cool.

Toss next 7 ingredients in large bowl.

Add chicken mixture to salad. Toss. Mix in tortilla
chips and dressing. Makes 10 cups (2.5 L).

1 cup (250 mL): 479 Calories; 33.5 g Total Fat;
3051 mg Sodium; 18 g Protein; 29 g Carbohydrate;
9 g Dietary Fiber

★★★★★★★★★★★★★★★★★★★★★★★★★★★★★★

FRUIT SALAD

A very fresh and colorful salad. Serve with dressing on the side.

DRESSING

Ripe avocado, peeled, pitted and mashed	1	1
Salad dressing (or mayonnaise)	⅔ cup	150 mL
Lemon juice	1 tbsp.	15 mL
Granulated sugar	1 tbsp.	15 mL

SALAD

Lettuce leaves	6	6
Medium pink grapefruit, peeled, cut into bite-size pieces	1	1
Papaya, peeled, cut into bite-size pieces	2	2
Can of pineapple chunks, drained, juice reserved	14 oz.	398 mL
Medium cooking apple (such as McIntosh), peeled and diced	1	1
Medium bananas, peeled and sliced	2	2
Reserved pineapple juice		
Medium pomegranate, seeds only		

Dressing: Combine all 4 ingredients in small bowl. Cover and chill until needed.

Salad: Line large glass bowl with lettuce leaves.

Combine next 3 ingredients in medium bowl. Toss.

Combine apple, banana and reserved juice in small bowl. Toss to coat. Drain well. Add to grapefruit mixture. Toss. Turn into lettuce-lined bowl.

Sprinkle with some pomegranate seeds. Put remaining seeds into small bowl. Serve salad with dressing on the side. Makes 8 cups (2 L).

1 cup (250 mL): 301 Calories; 19.9 g Total Fat; 108 mg Sodium; 2 g Protein; 32 g Carbohydrate; 4 g Dietary Fiber

MARINATED VEGETABLE SALAD

To obtain the more authentic zing to this dish simply omit the water when making the brine. Lots of color in this.

Small onion, cut into very thin rings	1	1
Cold water, to cover		
Cauliflower florets, cooked tender-crisp	¾ cup	175 mL
Sliced carrot, cooked tender-crisp	½ cup	125 mL
Thinly sliced celery	½ cup	125 mL
Short zucchini fingers	½ cup	125 mL
Slivered red pepper, cut matchstick size	½ cup	125 mL

BRINE

Water	1 cup	250 mL
White vinegar	1 cup	250 mL
Can of diced green chilies, with liquid	4 oz.	114 mL
Salt	½ tsp.	2 mL
Pepper	⅛ tsp.	0.5 mL
Dried whole oregano	½ tsp.	2 mL
Garlic powder	½ tsp.	2 mL

Put onion in cold water. Let stand for 1 hour. Drain.

Combine next 5 ingredients in bowl. Add onion.

Brine: Combine all 7 ingredients in small saucepan. Bring to a boil on medium. Simmer for 10 minutes. Pour over vegetables. Cool. Chill for 2 days to allow flavors to blend. Makes 8 cups (2 L).

1 cup (250 mL): 22 Calories; 0.1 g Total Fat; 281 mg Sodium; 1 g Protein; 6 g Carbohydrate; 1 g Dietary Fiber

CORN CHIP SALAD

Crunchy with the taste of corn chips. Chili powder adds an extra touch along with the dressing.

Small head of lettuce, cut or torn	1	1
Grated medium or sharp Cheddar cheese	2 cups	500 mL
Medium tomatoes, diced and drained on paper towel	2	2
Green onions, sliced	3-4	3-4
Can of ranch-style (or kidney) beans (14 oz., 398 mL), drained and rinsed	½	½
Chili powder	1 tsp.	5 mL
ISLAND DRESSING		
Cooking oil	1 tbsp.	15 mL
All-purpose flour	1 tbsp.	15 mL
Water	3 tbsp.	50 mL
White vinegar	2 tbsp.	30 mL
Granulated sugar	¼ cup	60 mL
Ketchup	2 tsp.	10 mL
Onion powder	⅛ tsp.	0.5 mL
Salt	⅛ tsp.	0.5 mL
Corn chips	3 cups	750 mL

Combine first 6 ingredients in large bowl. Toss.

Island Dressing: Stir cooking oil and flour in small saucepan until smooth.

Stir in next 6 ingredients. Heat and stir until boiling and thickened. Allow to cool thoroughly. Makes ½ cup (125 mL) dressing. Add to salad. Toss well to coat. Chill for 30 minutes.

Add corn chips just before serving. Toss. Makes 10 cups (2.5 L).

1 cup (250 mL): 258 Calories; 15.2 g Total Fat; 373 mg Sodium; 9 g Protein; 22 g Carbohydrate; 2 g Dietary Fiber

GUACAMOLE SALAD

Double duty. Use as a salad or as a spread for tortilla chips.

Envelopes of unflavored gelatin (¼ oz., 7 g, each)	2	2
Water	½ cup	125 mL
Lime juice	2 tbsp.	30 mL
Ripe small avocados, mashed smooth	3	3
Light sour cream	¾ cup	175 mL
Light salad dressing (or mayonnaise)	⅓ cup	75 mL
Spicy salsa, blended smooth	½ cup	125 mL
Salt	½ tsp.	2 mL
Garlic powder	¼ tsp.	1 mL
Hot pepper sauce (optional)	⅛ tsp.	0.5 mL
Cherry tomatoes, halved (optional)	3-4	3-4

Sprinkle gelatin over water in small saucepan. Let stand for 1 minute. Heat and stir until gelatin is dissolved.

Whisk next 8 ingredients together in medium bowl. Stir in gelatin mixture. If you have a 4 cup (1 L) mold with round indentations in bottom, place a cherry tomato half in each. Pour gelatin mixture over top. Chill for at least 2½ hours before removing from mold. Makes 4 cups (1 L).

2 tbsp. (30 mL): 45 Calories; 3.8 g Total Fat; 123 mg Sodium; 1 g Protein; 3 g Carbohydrate; 1 Dietary Fiber

Pictured on page 35.

Variation: If you don't have a mold with indentations, decorate top and sides with tomatoes after removing salad from mold.

MEXICAN SALAD

An uncommon salad with an excellent dressing.

Torn romaine lettuce, lightly packed	4 cups	1 L
Can of garbanzo beans (chick peas), drained and rinsed	14 oz.	398 mL
Ripe avocado, peeled, pitted and cut bite size (see Note)	1	1
DRESSING		
Granulated sugar	2 tbsp.	30 mL
White vinegar	1½ tbsp.	25 mL
Cooking oil	1 tbsp.	15 mL
Ketchup	1 tbsp.	15 mL
Onion powder	⅛ tsp.	0.5 mL
Worcestershire sauce	¼ tsp.	1 mL

Combine lettuce, garbanzo beans and avocado in large bowl.

Dressing: Mix all 6 ingredients with whisk. Pour over salad. Toss. Serves 4.

1 serving: 222 Calories; 12.4 g Total Fat; 170 mg Sodium; 6 g Protein; 25 g Carbohydrate; 4 g Dietary Fiber

Note: To prepare salad a short time ahead, dip avocado in lemon juice to prevent browning.

After washing salad greens, pat dry with paper towels to remove extra water. Chill for at least an hour before serving to ensure crispness.

SPINACH SALAD

Different and refreshing.

Large bundle of spinach leaves	1	1
Pink grapefruit, peeled and cut bite size	1	1
Can of garbanzo beans (chick peas), drained and rinsed	19 oz.	540 mL
Zucchini (7 inch, 18 cm), with peel, cut matchstick size	1	1
LIME DRESSING		
Salad dressing (or mayonnaise)	¼ cup	60 mL
Lime juice	1 tbsp.	15 mL
Granulated sugar	1 tbsp.	15 mL
Pine nuts	3 tbsp.	50 mL

Tear spinach leaves or leave whole and place in large bowl. Add grapefruit, garbanzo beans and zucchini.

Lime Dressing: Mix salad dressing, lime juice and sugar in small bowl. Stir. Pour over salad. Toss gently to coat.

Add pine nuts. Toss. Make 8 cups (2 L).

1 cup (250 mL): 123 Calories; 6.6 g Total Fat; 142 mg Sodium; 5 g Protein; 14 g Carbohydrate; 3 g Dietary Fiber

Pictured on page 53 and on back cover.

BASIL CREAM FIESTA

A cool refreshing salad on a warm summer day.

Tri-colored fusilli (spiral pasta), 8 oz. (225 g)	2⅔ cups	650 mL
Boiling water	3 qts.	3 L
Salt	1 tbsp.	15 mL
Broccoli florets	2 cups	500 mL
Cauliflower florets	2 cups	500 mL
Thinly sliced carrot	1 cup	250 mL
Diced green pepper	½ cup	125 mL
Diced red or yellow pepper	½ cup	125 mL
Green onions, sliced	2	2
Non-fat plain yogurt	½ cup	125 mL
Non-fat sour cream	½ cup	125 mL
White (or alcohol-free) wine	¼ cup	60 mL
Basil pesto	1 tbsp.	15 mL
Garlic clove, minced	1	1
Dry mustard	½ tsp.	2 mL
Dried whole oregano, crushed	½ tsp.	2 mL
Salt	1 tsp.	5 mL
Freshly ground pepper, sprinkle		

Cook pasta in boiling water and first amount of salt in large uncovered pot or Dutch oven for about 7 minutes, stirring occasionally, until tender but firm.

Add broccoli, cauliflower and carrot. Bring to a boil. Cook for 1 minute. Drain. Rinse with cold water. Drain. Place in large bowl.

Add peppers and green onion. Toss.

Combine remaining 9 ingredients in small bowl. Mix until smooth. Add to pasta mixture. Stir gently to coat. Cover. Chill. Makes 10 cups (2.5 L).

1 cup (250 mL): 129 Calories; 1.4 g Total Fat; 308 mg Sodium; 5 g Protein; 23 g Carbohydrate; 2 g Dietary Fiber

MEXICAN SALAD

A main meal salad. Add crusty brown dinner rolls and dig in.

Small head of iceberg lettuce, cut up	1	1
Grated medium Cheddar cheese	2 cups	500 mL
Can of kidney beans, drained and rinsed	14 oz.	398 mL
Small onion, diced or sliced	1	1
Medium tomatoes, diced or sliced	2	2
Catalina (or Russian) dressing	¾ cup	175 mL
Broken corn chips, for garnish	⅔ cup	150 mL

Put first 6 ingredients into medium bowl. Toss to coat.

Sprinkle chips over top. Makes 6 cups (1.5 L).

1 cup (250 mL): 393 Calories; 30.2 g Total Fat; 630 mg Sodium; 15 g Protein; 17 g Carbohydrate; 4 g Dietary Fiber

Soups

 ild or zippy, these hearty and delicious soups will fill you up and leave you craving a second helping. Since beans and lentils are so popular in Mexico, they form the basis for many soup recipes such as Garbanzo Soup, page 68. For a one-stop meal, try Tortilla Soup, page, 67, or Spicy Beef and Rice Soup, page 69.

PINTO TORTILLA SOUP

Rich and hearty-looking. Mild salsa adds taste.
A real winner.

Margarine (or butter)	1 tbsp.	15 mL
Chopped onion	½ cup	125 mL
Minced garlic	1 tsp.	5 mL
Water	3 cups	750 mL
Salsa	3 cups	750 mL
Cans of pinto beans (14 oz., 398 mL, each), with liquid	2	2
Chopped red pepper	½ cup	125 mL
Bay leaf	1	1
Vegetable bouillon powder	2 tbsp.	30 mL
Pepper	¼ tsp.	1 mL
GARNISH		
Flour tortillas, cut into 1½ x ¾ inch (3.8 x 2 cm) strips	2-3	2-3
Cooking oil, for deep-frying		
Grated medium Cheddar (or Monterey Jack) cheese (optional)	½ cup	125 mL

Melt margarine in saucepan. Add onion and garlic. Sauté until onion is soft.

Add next 7 ingredients. Cover. Simmer for 1 hour. Remove and discard bay leaf.

Garnish: Deep-fry tortilla strips in 375°F (190°C) cooking oil until browned. Remove with slotted spoon to paper towels to drain.

Add 1 tbsp. (15 mL) cheese and tortilla strips to each bowl of soup. Makes about 8½ cups (2.1 L).

1 cup (250 mL): 181 Calories; 3.8 g Total Fat; 688 mg Sodium; 8 g Protein; 29 g Carbohydrate; 5 g Dietary Fiber

Pictured on page 54.

WIENER AND LENTIL SOUP

A thick, yummy meal-type soup.

Green lentils	1 cup	250 mL
Water	5 cups	1.25 L
Salt	½ tsp.	2 mL
Margarine (or butter)	2 tbsp.	30 mL
Chopped onion	2 cups	500 mL
Grated carrot	1 cup	250 mL
Can of tomatoes, with juice, mashed	28 oz.	796 mL
Bay leaf	1	1
Garlic powder	½ tsp.	2 mL
Granulated sugar	½ tsp.	2 mL
Salt	1 tsp.	5 mL
Pepper	¼ tsp.	1 mL
Tofu wieners, cut into ¼ inch (6 mm) slices	6	6

Cook lentils in water and salt in saucepan for 30 to 40 minutes until tender. Drain. Reserve liquid.

Heat margarine in large saucepan. Add onion and carrot. Sauté until soft.

Add tomato, bay leaf, garlic powder, sugar, salt and pepper. Simmer for 30 minutes, stirring occasionally.

Add wieners and lentils. Heat through. Add about 2 cups (500 mL) reserved liquid for thinner consistency. Discard bay leaf. Makes 8 cups (2 L).

1 cup (250 mL): 201 Calories; 3.7 g Total Fat; 890 mg Sodium; 17 g Protein; 27 g Carbohydrate; 6 g Dietary Fiber

LENTIL SOUP

Light tan in color. Cooks faster than most soups. Good light flavor.

Water	6 cups	1.5 L
Chopped onion	1⅓ cups	325 mL
Red lentils	1⅓ cups	325 mL
Chopped celery	1 cup	250 mL
Salt	1 tsp.	5 mL
Pepper	¼ tsp.	1 mL
Garlic powder	¼ tsp.	1 mL
Instant vegetable stock mix	2 tbsp.	30 mL
Parsley flakes	1 tsp.	5 mL
Bay leaf, broken	1	1
Dried thyme	¼ tsp.	1 mL

Combine first 8 ingredients in large saucepan.

Place parsley flakes, bay leaf and thyme in tea ball or tie in double layer cheesecloth. Add to saucepan. Heat, stirring often, until boiling. Cover. Reduce heat. Simmer for about 30 minutes until vegetables are tender. Remove tea ball. Makes 7 cups (1.75 L).

1 cup (250 mL): 170 Calories; 1.5 g Total Fat; 621 mg Sodium; 12 g Protein; 29 g Carbohydrate; 6 g Dietary Fiber

Since dried beans, lentils and peas toughen with age, purchase in small quantities.

TORTILLA SOUP

This soup isn't complete without the tor-TEE-yah strips. They add lots of flavor.

Cooking oil	2 tbsp.	30 mL
Corn tortillas (6 inch, 15 cm, size)	5	5
Margarine (or butter)	1 tbsp.	15 mL
Chopped onion	¾ cup	175 mL
Shredded cooked chicken	2½ cups	625 mL
Water	8 cups	2 L
Can of diced green chilies, with liquid	4 oz.	114 mL
Chicken bouillon powder	3 tbsp.	50 mL
Parsley flakes	½ tsp.	2 mL
Salt	½ tsp.	2 mL

Heat cooking oil in frying pan until hot. Cut tortillas into ½ inch (12 mm) strips. Cut each strip into 2 or 3 pieces. Fry until crisp and browned. Remove with slotted spoon to paper towels to drain.

Melt margarine in large saucepan on medium. Add onion. Sauté until onion is clear and soft.

Add remaining 6 ingredients. Bring to a boil, stirring often. Cover. Reduce heat. Simmer gently for about 15 minutes. Ladle into 8 individual soup bowls. Add tortilla strips. Makes about 8 cups (2 L).

1 cup (250 mL): 195 Calories; 8.1 g Total Fat; 1094 mg Sodium; 17 g Protein; 13 g Carbohydrate; 1 g Dietary Fiber

To keep the skins on beans from splitting, cool in the cooking water, rather than draining and rinsing with water.

GARBANZO SOUP

This has its own good flavor. Great choice.

Chopped onion	1½ cups	375 mL
Cooking oil	2 tbsp.	30 mL
Can of diced tomatoes, with juice	14 oz.	398 mL
Ketchup	2 tbsp.	30 mL
Instant vegetable stock mix	2 tbsp.	30 mL
Dried whole oregano	1 tsp.	5 mL
Garlic powder	¼ tsp.	1 mL
Salt	½ tsp.	2 mL
Pepper	⅛ tsp.	0.5 mL
Cayenne pepper	⅛ tsp.	0.5 mL
Water	3 cups	750 mL
Can of garbanzo beans (chick peas), with liquid, puréed in blender	19 oz.	540 mL
Plain yogurt (or sour cream), for garnish	6 tbsp.	100 mL

Sauté onion in cooking oil in large saucepan until soft.

Add next 9 ingredients. Bring to a boil, stirring often. Boil gently for 15 minutes.

Add garbanzo beans. Stir. Bring to a boil. Reduce heat. Simmer for about 10 minutes to allow flavors to blend.

Ladle into 6 individual soup bowls. Garnish each serving with dollop of yogurt. Makes 6 cups (1.5 L).

1 cup (250 mL): 202 Calories; 7.7 g Total Fat; 658 mg Sodium; 7 g Protein; 28 g Carbohydrate; 4 g Dietary Fiber

CORN CHILI SOUP

Delicious soup with just the right amount of mild chili flavor.

Margarine (or butter)	2 tbsp.	30 mL
Chopped onion	¼ cup	60 mL
All-purpose flour	2 tbsp.	30 mL
Salt	1 tsp.	5 mL
Pepper	¼ tsp.	1 mL
Milk	4 cups	1 L
Chicken bouillon cubes (⅕ oz., 6 g, each)	2	2
Boiling water	1 cup	250 mL
Cans of cream-style corn (14 oz., 398 mL, each), smoothed in blender (see Note)	2	2
Can of diced green chilies, drained	3 tbsp.	50 mL
Sour cream, for garnish	½ cup	125 mL
Chopped green onion, for garnish	¼ cup	60 mL

Melt margarine in large saucepan. Add onion. Sauté until soft.

Mix in flour, salt and pepper. Stir in milk until boiling and thickened.

Dissolve bouillon cubes in boiling water. Add to milk mixture.

Stir in corn and chilies. Heat thoroughly. Pour into 8 individual soup bowls.

Mix sour cream and green onion together in small bowl. Garnish each serving with dollop of sour cream mixture. Makes about 8 cups (2 L).

1 cup (250 mL): 175 Calories; 5 g Total Fat; 1142 mg Sodium; 7 g Protein; 29 g Carbohydrate; 2 g Dietary Fiber

Pictured on page 54.

Note: Kernel corn may be smoothed in blender instead of using cream-style corn. Use 3½ to 4 cups (875 mL to 1 L).

MEXICAN SOUP

A different soup. The green chilies add spice but not too much heat. Most enjoyable.

Margarine (or butter)	2 tbsp.	30 mL
Chopped onion	1 cup	250 mL
Condensed chicken broth	2 cups	500 mL
Can of diced tomatoes, with juice	14 oz.	398 mL
Can of diced green chilies, with liquid	4 oz.	113 g
Monterey Jack cheese	4 oz.	113 g

Melt margarine in medium saucepan. Add onion. Sauté onion until soft.

Add broth, tomatoes with juice and green chilies with liquid. Simmer for 10 minutes until onion is cooked.

Cut in cheese. Stir to melt. Makes about 4¾ cups (1.2 L).

1 cup (250 mL): 184 Calories; 13 g Total Fat; 832 mg Sodium; 9 g Protein; 8 g Carbohydrate; 2 g Dietary Fiber

BLACK BEAN SOUP

Soup at its darkest. Mild and tasty. Easy to double or triple recipe.

Water	1½ cups	375 mL
Can of black beans, with liquid	19 oz.	540 mL
Instant vegetable stock mix	4 tsp.	20 mL
Ground coriander	¼ tsp.	1 mL
Ground cumin	¼ tsp.	1 mL
Sweet pickle relish	1 tsp.	5 mL
Hot pepper sauce	¼ tsp.	1 mL
Sour cream, for garnish	2 tbsp.	30 mL
Grated Monterey Jack cheese, for garnish	2 tsp.	10 mL

Process water and beans with liquid in blender. Pour into saucepan.

Add next 5 ingredients. Heat and stir until boiling. Reduce heat. Simmer, uncovered, for about 10 minutes to blend flavors.

Divide between 2 bowls. Top each with 1 tbsp. (15 mL) sour cream. Sprinkle each with 1 tsp. (5 mL) cheese. Makes 2 cups (500 mL).

1 cup (250 mL): 307 Calories; 3.5 g Total Fat; 509 mg Sodium; 18 g Protein; 52 g Carbohydrate; 9 g Dietary Fiber

To make beans easier to digest, discard water in which they have soaked and cook in fresh water.

SPICY BEEF AND RICE SOUP

Omit the chilies for a milder flavor.

Minute steaks	1 lb.	454 g
Cooking oil	2 tsp.	10 mL
Garlic clove, minced	1	1
Finely chopped onion	¼ cup	60 mL
Chopped fresh sweet basil	2 tbsp.	30 mL
Dried whole oregano	½ tsp.	2 mL
Dried thyme	¼ tsp.	1 mL
Dried crushed chilies	¼ tsp.	1 mL
Salt	½ tsp.	2 mL
Pepper	⅛ tsp.	0.5 mL
Water	5 cups	1.25 L
Can of diced Mexican-style tomatoes, drained	14 oz.	398 mL
Long grain white rice, uncooked	½ cup	125 mL
Chili powder	¼ tsp.	1 mL
Hot pepper sauce, to taste		
Chopped fresh cilantro	2 tbsp.	30 mL

Cut steaks into 1 inch (2.5 cm) strips, then across into 1 inch (2.5 cm) cubes. Heat cooking oil in non-stick frying pan. Add steak, garlic and onion. Sauté just until steak changes color. Turn into small bowl.

Sprinkle with basil, oregano, thyme, chilies, salt and pepper. Cover. Set aside.

Combine water, tomatoes, rice, chili powder and hot pepper sauce in large uncovered pot or Dutch oven. Bring to a boil. Reduce heat. Cover tightly. Simmer for 20 minutes. Add steak. Heat thoroughly. Gently stir in cilantro. Makes 8 cups (2 L).

1 cup (250 mL): 157 Calories; 5.4 g Total Fat; 402 mg Sodium; 14 g Protein; 12 g Carbohydrate; trace Dietary Fiber

Main Courses

Ⓨou don't need to wear a sombrero when you dine Mexican, but you'll feel like you should be when you dig into one of these entrees. Tortillas, cheese and chilies can be combined with beef or chicken and vegetables in a multitude of ways every day of the week. Put pasta to a unique and flavorful use in Chicken Fajita Pasta, page 80, or make a barbecue sizzle with Salsa-Stuffed Steak, page 92. For a dinnertime that deserves sharing try Tamale Pizza, page 94, or Chicken Enchiladas, page 98.

HAM MOLE

Sauce also goes well with chicken.

Can of pitted cherries, with juice	14 oz.	398 mL
Apple cider vinegar	2 tsp.	10 mL
Ground cloves	¹⁄₁₆ tsp.	0.5 mL
Semisweet chocolate chips	30	30
Cornstarch	1 tbsp.	15 mL
Water	2 tbsp.	30 mL
Ham steak	2¼ lbs.	1 kg

Combine cherries with juice, vinegar, cloves and chocolate chips in medium saucepan. Heat and stir until boiling.

Mix cornstarch and water in small cup. Stir into cherry mixture. Heat and stir until boiling and thickened.

Brown ham steak lightly on both sides in frying pan. Serve with sauce on top or separately. Serves 6.

1 serving: 264 Calories; 7.7 g Total Fat; 2118 mg Sodium; 33 g Protein; 14 g Carbohydrate; 1 g Dietary Fiber

Pictured on page 89.

1. Mexican Pasta Casserole, page 76
2. Chicken Fajita Pasta, page 79
3. Mexican Chicken Rolls, page 78

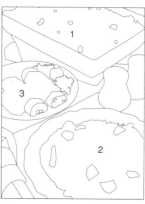

Props Courtesy Of: The Bay

★★★★★★★★★★★★★★★★★★★★★★★★★★★★★★★★

SPARERIBS MOLE

A dark sauce adds additional flavor to these tender ribs.

Pork spareribs, cut into 3-rib sections	3 lbs.	1.4 kg
Water, to cover		
Can of tomato sauce	7½ oz.	213 mL
White vinegar	2 tsp.	10 mL
Brown sugar, packed	3 tbsp.	50 mL
Onion powder	½ tsp.	2 mL
Ground ginger	¼ tsp.	1 mL
Garlic powder	¼ tsp.	1 mL
Cocoa, sifted if lumpy	1 tbsp.	15 mL
Liquid smoke	¼ tsp.	1 mL

Simmer spareribs in water for about 1 hour until tender. Drain. Spread on greased baking sheet.

Combine remaining 8 ingredients in small saucepan. Bring to a boil. Boil gently, stirring occasionally, for about 10 minutes until reduced and thickened. Brush on ribs. Bake in 400°F (205°C) oven for 8 to 10 minutes. Turn ribs. Brush with sauce. Bake for 8 to 10 minutes. Discard any remaining sauce. Serves 6.

1 serving: 289 Calories; 20.3 g Total Fat; 297 mg Sodium; 21 g Protein; 5 g Carbohydrate; 1 g Dietary Fiber

MEATLOAF MOLE

Looks great. Loaf holds together well. Cocoa enhances the flavor slightly without overpowering it.

Large eggs	2	2
Envelope of dry onion soup mix (1.4 oz., 38 g), stir before dividing	½	½
Water	½ cup	125 mL
Dry bread crumbs	½ cup	125 mL
Cocoa, sifted if lumpy	4 tsp.	20 mL
Celery salt	¼ tsp.	1 mL
Salt	½ tsp.	2 mL
Pepper	¼ tsp.	1 mL
Lean ground beef	2 lbs.	900 g
Ketchup	2 tbsp.	30 mL

Beat eggs in large bowl. Add next 7 ingredients. Stir.

Mix in ground beef. Pack into ungreased 9 x 5 x 3 inch (22 x 12.5 x 7.5 cm) loaf pan.

Spread with ketchup. Bake in 350°F (175°C) oven for about 1¼ hours. Serves 8.

1 serving: 310 Calories; 18.9 g Total Fat; 833 mg Sodium; 24 g Protein; 10 g Carbohydrate; 1 g Dietary Fiber

Pictured on page 117.

1. Tamale Pizza, page 94, with Confetti Biscuit Crust, page 94
2. Sopaipillas, page 115
3. Mexi-Beef Pitas, page 76
4. Nacho Pizza, page 57

CHILI MOLE

A dark, rich color. More chili powder can be added if desired.

Lean ground beef	1 lb.	454 g
Chopped onion	1 cup	250 mL
Can of condensed tomato soup	10 oz.	284 mL
Can of kidney beans, with liquid	14 oz.	398 mL
Grated carrot	½ cup	125 mL
Water	1 cup	250 mL
Beef bouillon powder	1 tsp.	5 mL
Worcestershire sauce	1 tsp.	5 mL
Salt	½ tsp.	2 mL
Pepper	¼ tsp.	1 mL
Liquid smoke	¼ tsp.	1 mL
Chili powder	2 tsp.	10 mL
Cocoa, sifted if lumpy	1 tbsp.	15 mL

Scramble-fry ground beef and onion in non-stick frying pan until beef is no longer pink and onion is soft. Drain. Turn into large saucepan.

Add remaining 11 ingredients. Stir well. Bring to a boil. Cover. Reduce heat. Simmer for about 15 minutes, stirring occasionally, until carrot is tender. Serves 6.

1 serving: 228 Calories; 7.6 g Total Fat; 976 mg Sodium; 19 g Protein; 22 g Carbohydrate; 6 g Dietary Fiber

CHICKEN WITH MOLE SAUCE

A good Mexican dish. Spicy hot moh-LAY sauce contains chocolate.

Chicken parts	6 lbs.	2.7 kg
Salt	1 tsp.	5 mL
Medium onion, quartered	1	1
Water, to cover		

Large green pepper, chopped	1	1
Chopped onion	½ cup	125 mL
Garlic cloves, halved	2	2
Can of diced tomatoes, with juice	14 oz.	398 mL
Raisins	⅓ cup	75 mL
Blanched almonds	¼ cup	60 mL
Toasted sesame seeds	2 tbsp.	30 mL
Ground cinnamon	¼ tsp.	1 mL
Ground cloves	⅛ tsp.	0.5 mL
Bread slices, toasted, dried and broken up	2	2
Semisweet chocolate baking square (1 oz., 28 g)	½	½
Cooking oil	2 tbsp.	30 mL
All-purpose flour	¼ cup	60 mL
Dried crushed chilies	1 tbsp.	15 mL
Salt	1 tsp.	5 mL
Pepper	¼ tsp.	1 mL
Toasted sesame seeds	2 tbsp.	30 mL

Place chicken, first amount of salt and onion in water in large pot or Dutch oven. Cover. Bring to a boil. Boil gently for about 1 hour until chicken is tender. Drain, reserving 4 cups (1 L) broth.

Measure next 11 ingredients into blender or food processor. Process until smooth.

Heat cooking oil in large saucepan on medium. Mix in flour, chilies, second amount of salt and pepper until smooth. Stir in reserved broth. Heat and stir until boiling and thickened. Add contents of blender. Stir. Add chicken. Simmer to heat through.

To serve, sprinkle with second amount of sesame seeds. Serves 8.

1 serving: 368 Calories; 14.7 g Total Fat; 862 mg Sodium; 40 g Protein; 20 g Carbohydrate; 3 g Dietary Fiber

Mole (moh-Lay) Sauce

This Mexican sauce includes a bit of cocoa or chocolate as a subtle flavor under the spiciness of chilies. Where you expect it to be sweet, instead the chocolate lends richness. Traditionally it's served with meat but it can also be served with beans.

CHICKEN MOLE

Serve this different dish to your next company. They'll never believe it contains chocolate.

Boneless, skinless chicken breast halves (about 6), pounded flat	1½ lbs.	680 g
Hard margarine	1 tbsp.	15 mL
Medium onion, chopped	1	1
Water	2 cups	500 mL
Can of diced green chilies, with liquid	4 oz.	114 mL
Sliced almonds, toasted	⅓ cup	75 mL
Chicken bouillon powder	2 tsp.	10 mL
Chili powder	2 tsp.	10 mL
Granulated sugar	1 tsp.	5 mL
Salt	1 tsp.	5 mL
Pepper	¼ tsp.	1 mL
Garlic powder (optional)	¼ tsp.	1 mL
Ground cinnamon	⅛ tsp.	0.5 mL
Ground cloves, just a pinch		
Unsweetened chocolate baking square, cut up	1 oz.	28 g
Long grain white rice	1⅓ cups	325 mL
Water	2⅔ cups	650 mL
Salt	½ tsp.	2 mL
Medium tomatoes, seeded and diced	2	2

Brown chicken on both sides in margarine in frying pan. Remove with slotted spoon to dish. Keep warm.

Add onion to frying pan. Sauté until golden.

Add next 12 ingredients. Stir. Add chicken. Cover. Simmer for 30 minutes until chicken is cooked. Remove chicken. Bring sauce to a boil. Boil, uncovered, for 10 minutes to thicken and slightly reduce. Slice chicken. Return to sauce.

Combine rice in second amounts of water and salt in medium saucepan. Cover. Simmer for 15 to 20 minutes until tender and moisture is absorbed.

Spread rice on platter. Spoon chicken mixture on top. Sprinkle with tomato. Serves 6.

1 serving: 390 Calories; 9.6 g Total Fat; 1140 mg Sodium; 33 g Protein; 43 g Carbohydrate; 3 g Dietary Fiber

MEXICAN PASTA CASSEROLE

The corn-flavored pasta gives this dish a Mexican kick.

Corn-flavored rotini (spiral pasta), 10 oz. (285 g)	4½ cups	1.1 L
Boiling water	3 qts.	3 L
Salt	1 tbsp.	15 mL
Lean ground beef	¾ lb.	340 g
Garlic cloves, minced	2	2
Medium onions, halved lengthwise and sliced	2	2
Chopped green or red pepper	1 cup	250 mL
Can of kernel corn, drained (or 1 cup, 250 mL, frozen, thawed)	12 oz.	341 mL
Can of diced green chilies, drained	4 oz.	114 mL
Can of crushed tomatoes	14 oz.	398 mL
Can of black beans, drained and rinsed	19 oz.	540 mL
Ground cumin	¼ tsp.	1 mL
Ground coriander	¼ tsp.	1 mL
Dried crushed chilies	⅛ tsp.	0.5 mL
Salt	½ tsp.	2 mL
Pepper	⅛ tsp.	0.5 mL
Grated light Monterey Jack cheese	1 cup	250 mL

Cook pasta in boiling water and first amount of salt in large uncovered pot or Dutch oven for 8 to 10 minutes, stirring occasionally, until tender but firm. Drain. Rinse with warm water. Drain. Return to pot.

Scramble-fry ground beef, garlic, onion and green pepper in large non-stick frying pan until beef is no longer pink. Drain. Add to pasta. Mix well.

Add next 9 ingredients. Mix well. Pour into greased 4 quart (4 L) casserole. Cover. Bake in 350°F (175°C) oven for 30 minutes.

Sprinkle cheese over top. Bake, uncovered, for 10 minutes until bubbling and cheese is melted. Serves 6.

1 serving: 471 Calories; 9.6 g Total Fat; 672 mg Sodium; 29 g Protein; 69 g Carbohydrate; 6 g Dietary Fiber

Pictured on page 71.

MEXI-BEEF PITAS

A great kids' lunch or after-school snack. Make the filling ahead and keep on hand.

Pita breads (3 inch, 7.5 cm, size)	10	10
FILLING		
Lean ground beef	1 lb.	454 g
Finely chopped onion	½ cup	125 mL
Can of pinto beans, drained	14 oz.	398 mL
Diced green pepper	½ cup	125 mL
Diced red pepper	¼ cup	60 mL
Chili powder	2 tsp.	10 mL
Salt	1 tsp.	5 mL
Grated Monterey Jack cheese	¾ cup	175 mL

Place pita bread in 300°F (150°C) oven to warm.

Filling: Scramble-fry ground beef in non-stick frying pan until no longer pink. Drain.

Add next 6 ingredients. Mix well. Heat for 2 to 3 minutes.

Remove pita breads from oven. Make slit in seam of each pita. Open pocket. Spoon in filling. Sprinkle with cheese. Place on ungreased baking sheet. Bake in oven until cheese is melted. Makes 10 mini pita sandwiches.

1 pita sandwich: 190 Calories; 6.8 g Total Fat; 519 mg Sodium; 14 g Protein; 18 g Carbohydrate; trace Dietary Fiber

Pictured on page 72.

MEXICAN CORN CHIP CASSEROLE

Use less jalapeño pepper or omit altogether if you need to keep the heat down.

Lean ground beef	1 lb.	454 g
Garlic clove, minced	1	1
Chopped onion	½ cup	125 mL
Chopped green pepper	½ cup	125 mL
Chopped fresh parsley	½ cup	125 mL
Medium tomatoes, diced	3	3
Can of tomato sauce	7½ oz.	213 mL
Fresh (or canned) jalapeño pepper, finely diced (see Tip, page 15)	1	1
Ground cumin	1 tsp.	5 mL
Chili powder	¼ tsp.	1 mL
Can of pinto beans, drained and rinsed	14 oz.	398 mL
Broken corn chips	2 cups	500 mL
Grated Monterey Jack cheese	½ cup	125 mL
Grated medium Cheddar cheese	½ cup	125 mL

Scramble-fry ground beef, garlic, onion, green pepper and parsley in large non-stick frying pan for about 5 minutes until beef is no longer pink. Drain.

Add tomato, tomato sauce and jalapeño pepper. Sauté until jalapeño pepper is soft.

Add cumin and chili powder. Simmer for 10 minutes, stirring occasionally. Remove from heat.

Add pinto beans. Stir. Pour into lightly greased 2 quart (2 L) casserole.

Sprinkle corn chips and both cheeses over top. Bake, uncovered, in 350°F (175°C) oven for 30 minutes. Serves 6.

1 serving: 387 Calories; 19.5 g Total Fat; 618 mg Sodium; 24 g Protein; 30 g Carbohydrate; 4 g Dietary Fiber

CHICKEN TACO CASSEROLE

The choice is yours to use mild or hot enchilada sauce. Crunchy topped.

Chicken parts Water, to cover	3 lbs.	1.4 kg
Corn chips	2 cups	500 mL
Can of enchilada sauce	10 oz.	284 mL
Can of condensed cream of mushroom soup	10 oz.	284 mL
Chopped onion	1½ cups	375 mL
Garlic salt	½ tsp.	2 mL
Grated Monterey Jack cheese	1 cup	250 mL
Corn chips	2 cups	500 mL

Put chicken into water in large saucepan. Cover. Bring to a boil. Cook for about 45 minutes until tender. Drain chicken, reserving 1 cup (250 mL) broth. Cool chicken enough to handle. Remove skin and bones. Cut chicken into bite-size pieces. Makes about 3½ cups (875 mL).

Scatter first amount of corn chips in 9 x 9 inch (22 x 22 cm) baking dish.

Combine next 4 ingredients in large bowl. Add chicken. Stir well. Spoon over corn chips in dish.

Sprinkle with cheese and second amount of corn chips. Pour reserved chicken broth over all. Bake, uncovered, in 350°F (175°C) oven for 45 to 60 minutes. Serves 6 to 8.

1 serving: 570 Calories; 28.7 g Total Fat; 1787 mg Sodium; 34 g Protein; 44 g Carbohydrate; 4 g Dietary Fiber

Pictured on page 36.

CHILI PEPPER PASTA DOUGH

A subtle hint of heat.

All-purpose flour (or durum semolina)	2 cups	500 mL
Salt	1 tsp.	5 mL
Dried crushed chilies	2 tsp.	10 mL
Frozen egg product, thawed	⅓ cup	75 mL
Tomato juice (or water), approximately	⅓ cup	75 mL

Combine flour, salt and chilies in food processor or large bowl.

Combine egg product and tomato juice in small cup. Gradually add through tube of food processor, while processing, until mixture forms ball. Or gradually mix into flour mixture in bowl until soft ball forms. Add bit more tomato juice if dough is too dry. Turn out onto lightly floured surface. Knead until smooth. Cover with plastic wrap. Let rest for 30 minutes. Makes 1 lb. (454 g) uncooked pasta.

3 oz. (85 g) uncooked pasta: 193 Calories; 0.7 g Total Fat; 596 mg Sodium; 7 g Protein; 39 g Carbohydrate; 2 g Dietary Fiber

Pictured on page 71.

MEXICAN CHICKEN ROLLS

Thick, creamy white sauce. So very rich, yet low in fat!

Can of skim evaporated milk	13½ oz.	385 mL
Skim milk	½ cup	125 mL
All-purpose flour	¼ cup	60 mL
Non-fat ranch dressing	½ cup	125 mL
Grated light Parmesan cheese	¼ cup	60 mL
Grated light Monterey Jack cheese	1 cup	250 mL
Salsa	¼ cup	60 mL
Can of diced green chilies, drained	4 oz.	114 mL
Diced cooked chicken (or turkey)	2½ cups	625 mL
Prepared Chili Pepper Pasta Dough, this page	1 lb.	454 g
Water	4 tbsp.	60 mL
Grated light Cheddar cheese	½ cup	125 mL

Gradually whisk both milks into flour in large saucepan until smooth. Whisk in dressing. Cook on medium, stirring often, until boiling and thickened. Remove from heat.

Stir in Parmesan and Monterey Jack cheeses until melted. Reserve 1½ cups (375 mL).

Stir salsa, green chilies and chicken into remaining sauce in saucepan.

Roll out ⅓ of rested pasta dough into 11 x 11 inch (28 x 28 cm) rectangle on lightly floured surface. Trim edges using ruler and sharp knife to make 10 x 10 inch (25 x 25 cm) rectangle. Cut straight line through center lengthwise and then crosswise to make four 5 x 5 inch (12.5 x 12.5 cm) squares. Spoon scant ⅓ cup (75 mL) filling in center of each square. Moisten 1 edge with water. Lift edges of dough over to form a roll and seal. Repeat until all dough and filling are used. Keep pasta covered with tea towel until ready to cook.

Pour 2 tbsp. (30 mL) water into lightly greased large shallow casserole dish or 9 x 13 inch (22 x 33 cm) baking dish. Lay rolls, seam side down, in single layer. Pour remaining 2 tbsp. (30 mL) water over rolls. Cover. Bake in 350°F (175°C) oven for 15 minutes. Pour reserved sauce over rolls. Sprinkle with Cheddar cheese. Cover. Bake in 350°F (175°C) oven for 15 minutes until cheese is melted. Makes 12 rolls.

1 roll: 246 Calories; 4.2 g Total Fat; 688 mg Sodium; 22 g Protein; 29 g Carbohydrate; 1 g Dietary Fiber

Pictured on page 71.

★★★★★★★★★★★★★★★★★★★★★★★★★★★★★★★★★

CHICKEN FAJITA PASTA

*Using a cast-iron frying pan sears the chicken
wonderfully and gives this dish its delicious flavor.*

Beer (or water)	½ cup	125 mL
Juice and grated peel of 1 small lime		
Lemon juice	1 tbsp.	15 mL
Garlic cloves, minced	2	2
Dried whole oregano	1 tsp.	5 mL
Onion powder	½ tsp.	2 mL
Ground cumin	¼ tsp.	1 mL
Dried crushed chilies	½ tsp.	2 mL
Coarsely ground pepper	¼ tsp.	1 mL
Boneless, skinless chicken breast halves (about 4)	1 lb.	454 g
Salt	½ tsp.	2 mL
Granulated sugar, just a pinch		
Cooking oil	1 tsp.	5 mL
Cooking oil	1 tsp.	5 mL
Medium red onion, cut in half lengthwise and thinly sliced	1	1
Medium green, red, orange or yellow peppers,sliced into thin slivers	2	2
Medium tomatoes, seeded and diced	2	2
Angel hair (very thin string) pasta (capellini)	10 oz.	285 g
Boiling water	3 qts.	3 L
Salt	1 tbsp.	15 mL

Combine first 9 ingredients in small bowl. Pour ½ of beer mixture into 10 inch (25 cm) glass pie plate. Add chicken. Turn to coat. Marinate at room temperature for 30 minutes.

Sprinkle first amount of salt and sugar over remaining ½ of beer mixture in bowl. Stir to dissolve.

Heat large cast-iron frying pan on medium until hot. Add first amount of cooking oil. Place chicken in single layer in frying pan. Spoon 2 tbsp. (30 mL) marinade over chicken, discarding remaining marinade. Cover. Cook for 5 minutes. Turn chicken over. Cover. Cook for 5 minutes. Turn chicken over. Cook for 2 to 3 minutes until well browned and no longer pink. Cut chicken crosswise into thin slices. Place chicken slices and any liquid on plate. Cover to keep warm.

Add second amount of cooking oil to hot frying pan. Add onion and green pepper. Stir-fry for 1 minute. Pour in remaining beer mixture. Stir-fry for 1 minute, while scraping up any bits from frying pan. Add chicken and liquid. Add tomato. Stir until tomato is hot. Remove to large serving bowl.

Cook pasta in boiling water and second amount of salt in large uncovered pot or Dutch oven for about 5 minutes, stirring occasionally, until tender but firm. Drain. Rinse with hot water. Drain. Pour over chicken mixture. Toss well to coat. Serves 6.

1 serving: 312 Calories; 3.5 g Total Fat; 285 mg Sodium; 25 g Protein; 43 g Carbohydrate; 3 g Dietary Fiber

Pictured on page 71.

CHICKEN FAJITA DINNER

Everyone in the family will like this one. A very child-friendly meal.

Lime juice	2 tbsp.	30 mL
Garlic cloves, minced (or ½ tsp., 2 mL, garlic powder)	2	2
Dried crushed chilies, finely crushed	¼ tsp.	1 mL
Salt	¼ tsp.	1 mL
Pepper, sprinkle		
Boneless, skinless chicken breast halves (about 4), cut into thin strips	1 lb.	454 g
Cooking oil	2 tsp.	10 mL
Small red (or other mild) onions, sliced and separated into rings	2	2
Medium green or yellow pepper, slivered	1	1
Medium red pepper, slivered	1	1
Frozen kernel corn, thawed	1 cup	250 mL
Chunky salsa	1 cup	250 mL
Water	2 tsp.	10 mL
Cornstarch	1 tsp.	5 mL
Corn chips (optional)	2 cups	500 mL

Put first 5 ingredients into medium bowl. Stir together well. Add chicken strips. Stir. Cover. Marinate in refrigerator for 1 to 2 hours.

Heat cooking oil in large frying pan. Add chicken and marinade. Stir-fry for about 3 minutes.

Add red onion and green and red peppers. Stir together. Cover. Cook, stirring occasionally, for about 4 minutes.

Add corn and salsa. Stir. Cook, uncovered, stirring occasionally, until hot and bubbling.

Mix water and cornstarch in small cup. Stir into boiling mixture until thickened.

Sprinkle with corn chips. Makes 6½ cups (1.6 L).

1½ cups (375 mL): 219 Calories; 3.9 g Total Fat; 1128 mg Sodium; 27 g Protein; 23 g Carbohydrate; 3 g Dietary Fiber

CHICKEN CHILI

This is a medium-flavored chili. Add more chili powder, to taste, if you like.

Cooking oil	2 tbsp.	30 mL
Chopped onion	2 cups	500 mL
Lean ground chicken	2 lbs.	900 g
All-purpose flour	2 tbsp.	30 mL
Can of diced tomatoes, with juice	14 oz.	398 mL
Cans of kidney beans (14 oz., 398 mL, each), with liquid	2	2
Chili powder	1 tbsp.	15 mL
Beef bouillon powder	1 tbsp.	15 mL
Salt	1 tsp.	5 mL
Pepper	¼ tsp.	1 mL
Dried whole oregano	¼ tsp.	1 mL
Granulated sugar	½ tsp.	2 mL
Worcestershire sauce	½ tsp.	2 mL

Heat cooking oil in frying pan. Add onion and ground chicken. Scramble-fry until chicken is no longer pink and onion is soft.

Mix in flour. Stir in tomatoes with juice until boiling.

Put remaining 8 ingredients into large uncovered pot or Dutch oven. Add chicken mixture. Stir. Bring to a boil. Reduce heat. Simmer for 30 minutes, stirring often. Makes about 8 cups (2 L).

1½ cups (375 mL): 442 Calories; 8.9 g Total Fat; 1730 mg Sodium; 52 g Protein; 38 g Carbohydrate; 13 g Dietary Fiber

★★★★★★★★★★★★★★★★★★★★★★★★★★★★★★

CHICK 'N' CHILI PENNE

Chili served over pasta. Very colorful.

Water	¼ cup	60 mL
Chicken bouillon powder	1 tsp.	5 mL
Chili powder	½ tsp.	2 mL
Ground cumin	¼ tsp.	1 mL
Cayenne pepper, sprinkle		
Boneless, skinless chicken breast halves (about 3), cut into ¾ inch (2 cm) cubes	¾ lb.	340 g
Diced onion	1½ cups	375 mL
Large carrot, grated	1	1
Diced green pepper	1½ cups	375 mL
Can of stewed tomatoes, with juice, chopped	14 oz.	398 mL
Can of kidney beans, with liquid	14 oz.	398 mL
Salt	½ tsp.	2 mL
Pepper, sprinkle		
Chili powder	½ tsp.	2 mL
Ground cumin	¼ tsp.	1 mL
Penne (medium tube pasta), 8 oz. (225 g)	2⅔ cups	650 mL
Boiling water	3 qts.	3 L
Salt	1 tbsp.	15 mL

Combine first 5 ingredients in large non-stick skillet. Bring to a boil.

Add chicken, onion and carrot. Cook, stirring often, until liquid is evaporated and chicken is no longer pink. Add green pepper. Cook for 2 minutes.

Add next 6 ingredients. Bring to a boil. Reduce heat. Simmer, uncovered, for 1 hour until thickened.

Cook pasta in boiling water and second amount of salt in large uncovered pot or Dutch oven for 10 minutes, stirring occasionally, until tender but firm. Drain. Serve chili over pasta. Serves 6.

1 serving: 312 Calories; 2 g Total Fat; 816 mg Sodium; 23 g Protein; 51 g Carbohydrate; 8 g Dietary Fiber

CHILI BEAN PASTA

Protein galore! And so very good. Add more chili powder if you like.

Margarine (or butter)	2 tbsp.	30 mL
Chopped onion	1¼ cups	300 mL
Chopped green pepper	⅓ cup	75 mL
Can of diced tomatoes, with juice	14 oz.	398 mL
Can of kidney beans, drained and rinsed	14 oz.	398 mL
Can of tomato sauce	7½ oz.	213 mL
Grated medium Cheddar cheese	2 cups	500 mL
Chili powder	2 tsp.	10 mL
Worcestershire sauce	1 tsp.	5 mL
Salt	½ tsp.	2 mL
Elbow macaroni	2 cups	500 mL
Boiling water	2½ qts.	2.5 L
Cooking oil (optional)	1 tbsp.	15 mL
Salt	2 tsp.	10 mL

Melt margarine in large saucepan. Add onion and green pepper. Sauté until soft.

Add next 7 ingredients. Heat and stir until simmering.

Cook macaroni in boiling water, cooking oil and second amount of salt in separate large uncovered saucepan for 5 to 7 minutes until tender but firm. Drain. Mix macaroni with sauce and serve. Makes about 10 cups (2.5 L).

1½ cups (375 mL): 380 Calories; 16.5 g Total Fat; 861 mg Sodium; 18 g Protein; 42 g Carbohydrate; 5 g Dietary Fiber

CHILI

Colorful, chunky, satisfying — and it's meatless!
Serve with crusty buns.

Cooking oil	2 tbsp.	30 mL
Chopped onion	3 cups	750 mL
Medium green pepper, chopped	1	1
Medium red pepper, chopped	1	1
Cans of kidney beans (14 oz., 398 mL, each), drained and rinsed	2	2
Can of pinto beans, drained and rinsed	14 oz.	398 mL
Medium eggplant, peeled and diced	1	1
Can of stewed tomatoes	14 oz.	398 mL
Can of condensed tomato soup	10 oz.	284 mL
Apple cider vinegar	1 tbsp.	15 mL
Brown sugar, packed	¼ cup	60 mL
Chili powder	2 tbsp.	30 mL
Can of sliced mushrooms, drained	10 oz.	284 mL
Garlic powder	½ tsp.	2 mL
Salt	1 tsp.	5 mL
Pepper	¼ tsp.	1 mL

Heat cooking oil in large frying pan. Add onion and peppers. Sauté until onion is soft.

Add remaining 12 ingredients. Bring to a boil, stirring often. Reduce heat. Simmer, uncovered, for 5 to 10 minutes, stirring occasionally. Makes about 10 cups (2.5 L).

1 cup (250 mL): 197 Calories; 4 g Total Fat; 807 mg Sodium; 8 g Protein; 36 g Carbohydrate; 7 g Dietary Fiber

CHILI CON CARNE

So handy and so stretchable. Simply add one
more can of beans.

Lean ground beef	1 lb.	454 g
Chopped onion	1 cup	250 mL
Cooking oil	2 tsp.	10 mL
Can of diced tomatoes, with juice	28 oz.	796 mL
Can of beans in tomato sauce	14 oz.	398 mL
Can of kidney beans, with liquid	14 oz.	398 mL
Chili powder	1-3 tsp.	5-15 mL
Worcestershire sauce	1 tsp.	5 mL
Granulated sugar	2 tsp.	10 mL
Salt	1 tsp.	5 mL
Pepper	¼ tsp.	1 mL

Scramble-fry ground beef and onion in cooking oil in large uncovered pot or Dutch oven until onion is soft and beef is no longer pink. Drain.

Add remaining 8 ingredients. Bring to a gentle boil, stirring often. Simmer, uncovered, stirring occasionally, until thickened. Add more chili powder according to taste. Makes about 5 cups (1.25 L).

1½ cups (375 mL): 448 Calories; 13.3 g Total Fat; 1878 mg Sodium; 34 g Protein; 53 g Carbohydrate, 18 g Dietary Fiber

Rinse canned beans with water before using, to reduce sodium and prevent the juice from discoloring the rest of the recipe.

Mexican

SPEEDY FAJITAS

Only 20 minutes from start to finish when you buy precut stir-fry strips.

Lime juice	1 tbsp.	15 mL
Chili powder	1 tbsp.	15 mL
Dried whole oregano	1 tsp.	5 mL
Garlic powder	½ tsp.	2 mL
Freshly ground pepper, to taste		
Beef stir-fry strips	1 lb.	454 g
Sliced fresh mushrooms	2 cups	500 mL
Medium red or green pepper, cut into strips	1	1
Green onions, cut into 1 inch (2.5 cm) pieces	4	4
Cooking oil	2 tsp.	10 mL
Flour tortillas (10 inch, 25 cm, size)	8	8
Salsa	½ cup	125 mL

Mix first 5 ingredients in medium bowl. Add beef strips. Stir to coat. Marinate at room temperature for 10 minutes.

Sauté mushrooms, pepper strips and green onion in cooking oil in frying pan for 2 to 3 minutes. Remove to bowl.

Wrap tortillas in damp tea towel. Warm in oven.

Stir-fry beef strips mixture in frying pan for 5 minutes until browned. Add to vegetable mixture. Stir. Put ½ cup (125 mL) onto each tortilla. Add 1 tbsp. (15 mL) salsa on each. Fold up bottom and then fold in sides, envelope-style, leaving top open. Makes 8 fajitas.

1 fajita: 242 Calories; 6.2 g Total Fat; 206 mg Sodium; 18 g Protein; 29 g Carbohydrate; 1 g Dietary Fiber

TURKEY FAJITAS

A fun way to use up leftover turkey.

Margarine (butter browns too fast)	1 tbsp.	15 mL
Large onion, thinly sliced	1	1
Medium green or yellow pepper, cut into strips	1	1
Medium red pepper, cut into strips	1	1
Margarine (or butter)	1 tbsp.	15 mL
Cooked turkey, cut into thin strips	3 cups	750 mL
Salt, sprinkle		
Pepper, sprinkle		
Seeded and diced tomato	1 cup	250 mL
Grated medium Cheddar cheese	1 cup	250 mL
Shredded lettuce, lightly packed	1 cup	250 mL
Sour cream	1 cup	250 mL
Salsa	1 cup	250 mL
Guacamole	1 cup	250 mL
Flour tortillas (8 inch, 20 cm, size), warmed (see Tip, page 85)	8-10	8-10

Melt first amount of margarine in frying pan. Add onion and peppers. Stir-fry until lightly browned.

Melt second amount of margarine in saucepan. Add turkey. Sprinkle with salt and pepper. Cover. Heat, stirring as little as possible so turkey doesn't break up.

Put next 6 ingredients into separate serving bowls.

Lay 1 tortilla on plate. Place some onion-pepper mixture down center. Add some turkey strips. Add any or all of 6 garnishes. Fold up bottom and then fold in sides, envelope-style, leaving top open. Makes 8 to 10 fajitas.

1 fajita: 501 Calories; 22.3 g Total Fat; 1048 mg Sodium; 29 g Protein; 47 g Carbohydrate; 3 g Dietary Fiber

CHICKEN FAJITAS

Preparation time is 25 minutes. A fun meal to eat with your hands.

Condensed chicken broth	¼ cup	60 mL
Lime juice	¼ cup	60 mL
Garlic cloves, crushed	2	2
Dried crushed chilies	½ tsp.	2 mL
Chili powder	½ tsp.	2 mL
Ground cumin (optional)	⅛ tsp.	0.5 mL
Boneless, skinless chicken breast halves (about 3)	¾ lb.	340 g
Large onion, thinly sliced into rings	1	1
Medium green pepper, thinly sliced	1	1
Medium red pepper, thinly sliced	1	1
Flour tortillas (8 inch, 20 cm, size), warmed (see Tip, page 85)	6	6
Non-fat sour cream (optional)		
Shredded lettuce (optional)		
Diced tomato (optional)		

Combine first 6 ingredients in medium bowl.

Add chicken. Turn to coat. Marinate at room temperature for 30 minutes. Heat lightly greased large non-stick frying pan until hot. Remove chicken from marinade, reserving marinade. Sear chicken in frying pan until browned.

Add onion, peppers and reserved marinade. Toss together. Cover. Cook for 7 minutes until vegetables are tender and chicken is no longer pink. Remove chicken. Slice thinly.

Place about ⅔ cup (150 mL) chicken and vegetables down center of each tortilla. Add sour cream, lettuce and tomato. Fold up bottom and then fold in sides, envelope-style, leaving top open. Makes 6 fajitas.

1 fajita: 252 Calories; 1.8 g Total Fat; 318 mg Sodium; 20 g Protein; 38 g Carbohydrate; 1 g Dietary Fiber

BARBECUED FAJITAS

Keep beef more rare than well done as flank steak is most tender that way.

MARINADE		
Lime juice	¼ cup	60 mL
Olive oil	1 tbsp.	15 mL
Dried whole oregano	1 tbsp.	15 mL
Dried crushed chilies	½ tsp.	2 mL
Salt	¼ tsp.	1 mL
Freshly ground pepper	⅛ tsp.	0.5 mL
Garlic cloves, crushed	2	2
Flank steak (scored on 1 side)	1½ lbs.	680 g
Flour tortillas (8 inch, 20 cm, size), warmed (see Tip, page 85)	8	8
Black Bean Salsa, page 40		
Chopped tomatoes (optional)		
Shredded lettuce (optional)		
Sliced avocados (optional)		
Sliced hot peppers (optional)		
Sliced green onions (optional)		

Marinade: Combine first 7 ingredients in shallow dish or resealable plastic bag. Place steak in marinade. Turn to coat. Cover or seal. Marinate in the refrigerator overnight, turning several times.

Remove steak. Discard marinade. Barbecue over medium for 5 to 7 minutes per side for medium or to desired doneness. Thinly slice steak diagonally across the grain. Fill warmed tortillas with steak and selected toppings. Fold up bottom and then fold in sides, envelope-style, leaving top open. Makes 8 fajitas.

1 fajita: 265 Calories; 7.2 g Total Fat; 214 mg Sodium; 23 g Protein; 25 g Carbohydrate; trace Dietary Fiber

BEEF FAJITAS

Once the chopping is done, the rest is fast and easy. Set everything out so everyone can assemble their own.

Sirloin steak, sliced into ⅛ inch (3 mm) thin strips	¾ lb.	340 g
Lemon juice	1 tbsp.	15 mL
Chili powder	½ tsp.	2 mL
Salt	½ tsp.	2 mL
Pepper	1/16 tsp.	0.5 mL
Cooking oil	1 tsp.	5 mL
Medium green pepper, cut into slivers	1	1
Medium red pepper, cut into slivers	1	1
Large onion, cut into slivers	1	1
Cooking oil	1 tbsp.	15 mL
Medium tomatoes, diced	2	2
Grated medium or sharp Cheddar cheese	½ cup	125 mL
Light sour cream	3 tbsp.	50 mL
Salsa	½ cup	125 mL
Shredded lettuce, lightly packed	1 cup	250 mL
Guacamole (optional)	½ cup	125 mL
Flour tortillas (8 inch, 20 cm, size), warmed (see Tip, this page)	8	8

Combine steak, lemon juice, chili powder, salt and pepper in small bowl. Marinate at room temperature for 10 minutes.

Heat first amount of cooking oil in frying pan or wok on medium-high. Add pepper strips and onion. Stir-fry for 4 minutes until soft. Transfer to separate bowl.

Add second amount of cooking oil to hot wok. Add beef strips. Stir-fry for about 4 minutes until desired doneness. Add pepper mixture. Stir to heat through.

Place next 6 ingredients in separate small bowls.

Divide strips of steak, peppers and onion among warmed tortillas. Add selected toppings. Fold up bottom and then fold in sides, envelope-style, leaving top open. Makes 8.

1 fajita: 237 Calories; 6.4 g Total Fat; 630 mg Sodium; 16 g Protein; 29 g Carbohydrate; 2 g Dietary Fiber

To warm and soften tortillas, wrap in foil or damp tea towel and heat in 200°F (95°C) oven for about 10 minutes.

QUICK TAMALE CASSEROLE

Get the tamale flavor the easy way.

Lean ground beef	1 lb.	454 g
Chopped onion	1 cup	250 mL
Can of diced tomatoes, with juice	14 oz.	398 mL
Yellow cornmeal	½ cup	125 mL
Kernel corn, fresh or frozen	1½ cups	375 mL
Chili powder	1 tsp.	5 mL
Salt	½ tsp.	2 mL
Pepper	¼ tsp.	1 mL

Spray frying pan with no-stick cooking spray. Add ground beef and onion. Sauté until onion is soft and beef is no longer pink. Drain.

Combine tomatoes with juice and cornmeal in large saucepan. Bring to a boil. Reduce heat. Simmer for 5 minutes, stirring occasionally.

Add remaining 4 ingredients. Add beef mixture. Stir. Turn into 2 quart (2 L) casserole. Bake, uncovered, in 350°F (175°C) oven for about 30 minutes. Serves 6.

1 serving: 223 Calories; 7.3 g Total Fat; 376 mg Sodium; 17 g Protein; 24 g Carbohydrate; 2 g Dietary Fiber

STEAK FAJITAS

Great with Guacamole, page 14. For those of you with indoor counter-top grills—enjoy!

Beer	½ cup	125 mL
Lime juice	¼ cup	60 mL
Water	¼ cup	60 mL
Garlic cloves, minced	2	2
Cajun seasoning	1-2 tsp.	5-10 mL
Freshly ground pepper, sprinkle		
Flank steak (scored on 1 side)	1¼ lbs.	560 g

Cooking oil	1 tbsp.	15 mL
Large onions, cut into ½ inch (12 mm) slices	2	2
Medium red pepper, quartered	1	1
Medium orange or yellow pepper, quartered	1	1
Flour tortillas (8 inch, 20 cm, size), warmed (see Tip, page 85)	8	8

Combine first 6 ingredients in small bowl.

Place steak in resealable plastic bag or shallow casserole. Pour ½ cup (125 mL) marinade over steak. Seal or cover. Chill for 6 hours or overnight. Drain and reserve marinade for basting. Preheat lightly sprayed electric grill to high. Sear steak in hot frying pan for 1 minute per side. Baste with reserved marinade. Cook on high for 10 minutes per side, basting occasionally.

Combine remaining ½ cup (125 mL) marinade with cooking oil.

Cook onion and both peppers on hot grill, turning and basting with oil mixture several times, until tender-crisp. Discard any remaining marinade. Remove vegetables to cutting board. Sliver peppers, cut onion slices into quarters and cut steak into thin slices on diagonal.

Divide steak and vegetables among warmed tortillas. Fold tortilla up from bottom and then fold in sides, envelope style, leaving top open. Makes 8 fajitas.

1 fajita: 313 Calories; 7.6 g Total Fat; 243 mg Sodium; 22 g Protein; 37 g Carbohydrate; 1 g Dietary Fiber

Pictured on page 53 and on back cover.

Tamale Pie

Make and bake in 1 hour. Just add a salad to complete this meal.

Lean ground beef	1½ lbs.	680 g
Garlic cloves, minced	2	2
Can of stewed tomatoes, with juice, chopped	28 oz.	796 mL
Chili powder	2 tsp.	10 mL
Salt	⅛ tsp.	0.5 mL
Freshly ground pepper	⅛ tsp.	0.5 mL
Chopped fresh parsley	¼ cup	60 mL

TOPPING

All-purpose flour	1 cup	250 mL
Cornmeal	¾ cup	175 mL
Granulated sugar	1 tbsp.	15 mL
Baking powder	2 tsp.	10 mL
Baking soda	½ tsp.	2 mL
Salt	½ tsp.	2 mL
Grated Parmesan cheese	3 tbsp.	50 mL
Large egg	1	1
1% buttermilk (or sour milk)	1 cup	250 mL
Cooking oil	¼ cup	60 mL
Dashes of hot pepper sauce	3	3

Scramble-fry ground beef and garlic in large non-stick frying pan until beef is no longer pink. Drain. Add tomatoes with juice and chili powder. Bring to a boil. Reduce heat. Simmer until mixture is consistency of thick spaghetti sauce. Add salt, pepper and parsley. Transfer to an ungreased deep 10 inch (25 cm) pie plate.

Topping: Stir flour, cornmeal, sugar, baking powder, baking soda and salt together in large bowl. Mix well. Add Parmesan cheese. Toss lightly.

Beat egg, buttermilk, cooking oil and hot pepper sauce together well in separate bowl. Add egg mixture to dry ingredients. Stir until dry ingredients are just moistened. Spread cornmeal mixture evenly on beef mixture. Bake in 375°F (190°C) oven for 30 minutes until the topping is golden. A wooden pick inserted in the center should come out clean. Serves 6.

1 serving: 486 Calories; 22 g Total Fat; 843 mg Sodium; 29 g Protein; 44 g Carbohydrate; 4 g Dietary Fiber

Tamale Pie

This is a real time saver, a lazy tamale. Meat filling sandwiched between layers of cornmeal batter.

FILLING

Cooking oil	1 tbsp.	15 mL
Ground beef	1 lb.	454 g
Chopped onion	1 cup	250 mL
Chopped green pepper	⅓ cup	75 mL
Garlic clove, minced	1	1
Can of diced tomatoes, with juice	14 oz.	398 mL
Chili powder	1 tbsp.	15 mL
Salt	1 tsp.	5 mL
Pepper	¼ tsp.	1 mL

CRUST

Cornmeal	2 cups	500 mL
Baking powder	1 tsp.	5 mL
Salt	½ tsp.	2 mL
Boiling water	5 cups	1.25 L

Filling: Heat cooking oil in frying pan. Add ground beef, onion, green pepper and garlic. Scramble-fry until beef is no longer pink and onion is soft. Drain.

Add next 4 ingredients. Bring to a boil. Reduce heat. Cover. Simmer for 45 minutes.

Crust: Combine all 4 ingredients in large saucepan. Heat and stir until boiling. Reduce heat. Simmer, uncovered, for about 15 minutes until thick but still pourable. Pour ½ of mixture into greased 8 x 8 inch (20 x 20 cm) baking dish. Spoon beef mixture over top. Cover with remaining crust mixture. Bake in 350°F (175°C) oven for about 45 minutes until browned and firm. Serves 8 generously.

1 serving: 259 Calories; 7.4 g Total Fat; 625 mg Sodium; 14 g Protein; 34 g Carbohydrate; 3 g Dietary Fiber

TAMALE CASSEROLE

Great for the buffet table.

Water	3¾ cups	925 mL
Salt	1½ tsp.	7 mL
Cornmeal	1 cup	250 mL
Chopped, pitted ripe olives	1 cup	250 mL
Margarine (butter browns too fast)	2 tbsp.	30 mL
Chopped onion	1 cup	250 mL
Medium green pepper, chopped	1	1
Lean ground beef	1 lb.	454 g
Salt	1 tsp.	5 mL
Can of diced tomatoes, with juice	14 oz.	398 mL
Chili powder	2 tsp.	10 mL
Cayenne pepper	¼ tsp.	1 mL

Bring water to boil in large saucepan. Add first amount of salt. Slowly stir cornmeal into boiling liquid. Heat and stir for 5 minutes.

Add olives. Stir.

Melt margarine in frying pan. Add onion, green pepper, ground beef and second amount of salt. Sauté until beef is no longer pink and onion and pepper are soft. Drain.

Add tomatoes, chili powder and cayenne pepper. Stir. Spread ½ of cornmeal mixture in greased 3 quart (3 L) casserole. Spread beef mixture on top. Spread second ½ of cornmeal mixture on meat. Bake, uncovered, in 350°F (175°C) oven for about 30 minutes until hot and lightly browned. Serves 6 to 8.

1 serving: 284 Calories; 12.4 g Total Fat; 1451 mg Sodium; 17 g Protein; 26 g Carbohydrate; 3 g Dietary Fiber

MEXICAN FLATBREAD PIZZA

As a variation, omit the flatbread and serve in taco shells or wrapped in tortillas.

Flatbread (or prebaked pizza crust), 12 inch (30 cm)	1	1
Minute (or fast-fry) steaks, ¼ inch (6 mm) thick	1 lb.	454 g
Chunky salsa	½ cup	125 mL
Lime juice	2 tbsp.	30 mL
Chunky salsa	½ cup	125 mL
Grated Monterey Jack cheese	¼ cup	60 mL
Grated medium Cheddar cheese	¼ cup	60 mL

Place flatbread on baking sheet in 200°F (95°C) oven.

Marinate steak in first amount of salsa and lime juice in medium bowl for 15 minutes. Remove steak and discard marinade. Cook steak in non-stick frying pan for about 2 minutes per side until desired doneness. Cut into thin strips.

Spread second amount of salsa on flatbread. Top with steak and sprinkle with both cheeses. Broil for 2 minutes until cheese is melted. Cuts into 8 wedges.

1 wedge: 237 Calories; 7.3 g Total Fat; 560 mg Sodium; 18 g Protein; 24 g Carbohydrate; 1 g Dietary Fiber

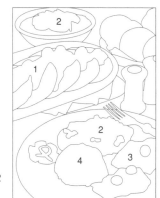

1. Ham Mole, page 70
2. Calabacitas, page 105
3. Red Snapper Veracruz-Style, page 92
4. Green Rice, page 105

Props Courtesy Of: The Bay

ARROZ CON POLLO

Pronounced ah-ROHS kahn POH-yoh and literally means "rice with chicken." A Spanish and Mexican dish.

Skinless bone-in chicken parts	**3½ lbs.**	**1.6 kg**
Long grain white rice, uncooked	**1½ cups**	**375 mL**
Finely chopped onion	**½ cup**	**125 mL**
Frozen peas, thawed	**2 cups**	**500 mL**
Chicken bouillon powder	**1 tbsp.**	**15 mL**
Salt	**1 tsp.**	**5 mL**
Pepper	**¼ tsp.**	**1 mL**
Saffron (or turmeric)	**¼ tsp.**	**1 mL**
Jar of chopped pimiento, drained	**2 oz.**	**57 mL**
Boiling water	**3 cups**	**750 mL**
Can of diced tomatoes, with juice	**14 oz.**	**398 mL**
Dried sweet basil	**½ tsp.**	**2 mL**
Garlic powder	**¼ tsp.**	**1 mL**

Arrange chicken in greased 9 x 13 inch (22 x 33 cm) baking dish. Bake, uncovered, in 350°F (175°C) oven for 30 minutes. Remove chicken to plate.

Stir remaining 12 ingredients together in same pan. Place chicken on rice mixture. Cover. Bake for 35 to 45 minutes until rice and chicken are tender. Serves 6.

1 serving: 395 Calories; 4.7 g Total Fat; 1050 mg Sodium; 35 g Protein; 51 g Carbohydrate; 4 g Dietary Fiber

Pictured on page 90.

EASY TACO SUPPER

Fast, easy and so good.

Lean ground beef	**1 lb.**	**454 g**
Chopped onion	**½ cup**	**125 mL**
Chopped green pepper	**½ cup**	**125 mL**
Hot water	**2½ cups**	**625 mL**
Envelope of taco seasoning mix	**1¼ oz.**	**35 g**
Package of macaroni and cheese dinner	**6½ oz.**	**200 g**
Diced tomato	**1 cup**	**250 mL**
Non-fat sour cream (optional)	**½ cup**	**125 mL**
Thinly sliced green onion (optional)	**¼ cup**	**60 mL**
Shredded lettuce (optional)	**2 cups**	**500 mL**

Scramble-fry ground beef, onion and green pepper in large non-stick frying pan for about 5 minutes until onion is soft and beef is no longer pink. Drain.

Stir in hot water and taco seasoning mix. Bring to a boil. Stir in macaroni from package, reserving cheese packet. Cover. Reduce heat. Simmer, stirring occasionally, for 7 to 8 minutes until macaroni is tender.

Add reserved cheese packet and tomato. Stir well.

Serve immediately with sour cream, green onion and lettuce. Serves 6.

1 serving: 275 Calories; 8.1 g Total Fat; 691 mg Sodium; 20 g Protein; 31 g Carbohydrate; 1 g Dietary Fiber

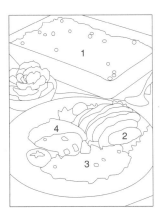

1. Arroz Con Pollo, above
2. Santa Fe Mushroom, page 104
3. Noodles Con Queso, page 110
4. Salsa-Stuffed Steak, page 92

Props Courtesy Of: The Bay

SALSA-STUFFED STEAK

The hotter the salsa the hotter the surprise. Prepare in 10 minutes.

Sirloin (or strip loin or rib-eye) steak, ¾ to 1 inch (2 to 2.5 cm) thick	**1½ lbs.**	**680 g**
Salsa	**½ cup**	**125 mL**
Garlic cloves, minced	**2**	**2**
Small onion, finely chopped	**1**	**1**
Ground cumin (or dried whole oregano)	**1 tsp.**	**5 mL**
Pepper	**1 tsp.**	**5 mL**

Salsa (optional)
Sour cream (optional)

Cut steak into 6 equal portions. Cut a deep horizontal pocket into 1 side of each piece.

Combine first amount of salsa, garlic and onion in small bowl. Stuff salsa mixture into each steak pocket. Close pocket with skewer. Sprinkle steaks with cumin and pepper. Barbecue over medium-low for 5 to 7 minutes per side for medium or to desired doneness.

Serve with more salsa and sour cream. Serves 4.

1 serving: 224 Calories; 6.4 Total Fat; 118 mg Sodium; 35 g Protein; 6 g Carbohydrate; 1 g Dietary Fiber

Pictured on page 90.

Leftover steak is great sliced thinly on the diagonal and served over salad.

RED SNAPPER VERACRUZ STYLE

A great make-ahead dish. When ready, just pour sauce over fish and bake.

Margarine (or butter)	**2 tbsp.**	**30 mL**
Chopped onion	**1 cup**	**250 mL**
Garlic clove, minced	**1**	**1**
Can of diced tomatoes, with juice	**14 oz.**	**398 mL**
Pimiento-stuffed green olives	**½ cup**	**125 mL**
Capers (optional)	**2 tbsp.**	**30 mL**
Bay leaf	**1**	**1**
Salt	**1 tsp.**	**5 mL**
Pepper	**¼ tsp.**	**1 mL**
Red snapper fillets	**3 lbs.**	**1.4 kg**

Lemon and lime wedges, for garnish

Melt margarine in large saucepan on medium. Add onion and garlic. Sauté until soft but not browned.

Add next 6 ingredients. Bring to a boil. Reduce heat. Simmer, uncovered, for 10 minutes. Discard bay leaf.

Cut fillets into serving-size pieces. Arrange in small greased roaster. Pour sauce over fish. Cover. Bake in 350°F (175°C) oven for 25 to 30 minutes until fish flakes when tested with fork.

Serve with lemon wedges. Serves 8.

1 serving: 225 Calories; 6.5 g Total Fat; 769 mg Sodium; 36 g Protein; 4 g Carbohydrate; 1 g Dietary Fiber

Pictured on page 89.

Paella

Spanish in origin, pie-AY-yuh is a terrific company casserole. Serve with green peas for color contrast.

Cooking oil	2 tbsp.	30 mL
Boneless skinless chicken breast halves (about 8)	2 lbs.	900 g
Chopped onion	1½ cups	375 mL
Garlic cloves, minced (or ½ tsp., 2 mL, garlic powder)	2	2
Chorizo (or other hot sausage), sliced ½ inch (12 mm) thick	¾ lb.	340 g
Water	4 cups	1 L
Can of stewed tomatoes	14 oz.	398 mL
Long grain white rice, uncooked	2 cups	500 mL
Chicken bouillon powder	4 tsp.	20 mL
Saffron (or turmeric)	¼ tsp.	1 mL
Salt	2 tsp.	10 mL
Pepper	½ tsp.	2 mL
Scallops (large ones cut in half)	1 lb.	454 g
Boiling water, to cover		
Medium uncooked shrimp, peeled and deveined	1 lb.	454 g
Boiling water, to cover		

Heat cooking oil in large uncovered pot or Dutch oven. Add chicken in 1 or 2 batches. Brown both sides quickly. It is not necessary to cook chicken through at this stage. Remove chicken to plate. Cut into bite-size pieces.

Combine onion, garlic and sausage in same pot, adding more cooking oil if needed. Sauté until onion is soft.

Add water, tomatoes, rice, bouillon powder, saffron, salt and pepper. Add chicken. Bring to a boil. Cover. Cook on medium for 15 to 20 minutes until rice is tender.

Cook scallops in first amount of boiling water in medium saucepan for 3 to 5 minutes until white and opaque. Drain. Add to chicken mixture.

Cook shrimp in second amount of boiling water in medium saucepan for about 1 minute until pinkish and curled. Drain. Add to chicken mixture. Serves 8.

1 serving: 671 Calories; 23.3 g Total Fat; 1866 mg Sodium; 63 g Protein; 47 g Carbohydrate; 2 g Dietary Fiber

Sausages will keep their size and not break if they are rolled lightly in flour prior to frying. This also works well for bacon.

Tamale Pizza

This is really different. Sure to please if you like tamales.

Cornmeal	**2 tsp.**	**10 mL**
Basic Pizza Crust dough, page 95 (or partially baked commercial crust)	**1**	**1**
Can of cream-style corn	**10 oz.**	**284 mL**
Cornstarch	**4 tsp.**	**20 mL**
Lean ground beef	**½ lb.**	**225 g**
Chopped onion	**½ cup**	**125 mL**
Chopped green pepper	**¼ cup**	**60 mL**
Can of diced tomatoes, well drained	**14 oz.**	**398 mL**
Chili powder	**1-1½ tsp.**	**5-7 mL**
Garlic powder	**¼ tsp.**	**1 mL**
Salt	**½ tsp.**	**2 mL**
Pepper	**⅛ tsp.**	**0.5 mL**
Cornmeal	**½ cup**	**125 mL**
Baking powder	**¼ tsp.**	**1 mL**
Salt	**¼ tsp.**	**1 mL**
Boiling water	**1¼ cups**	**300 mL**
Grated Monterey Jack cheese	**1½ cups**	**375 mL**
Sliced pitted ripe olives	**¼ cup**	**60 mL**

Sprinkle bottom of greased 12 inch (30 cm) pizza pan with first amount of cornmeal. Prepare pizza dough. Roll out large enough to fit pan. Place over cornmeal, forming rim around edge.

Mix corn and cornstarch in small saucepan. Heat and stir until boiling and thickened. Set aside.

Scramble-fry ground beef, onion and green pepper in large non-stick frying pan until onion is soft and beef is no longer pink. Drain.

Add next 5 ingredients. Mix well. Set aside.

Measure second amount of cornmeal, baking powder and second amount of salt into medium saucepan. Mix in boiling water. Heat and stir for about 5 minutes until very thick. Pour into greased 9 inch (22 cm) pie plate. Cool. Letting it stand in freezer or refrigerator will hurry the cooling. Turn out of pan. Cut into 8 wedges.

Spread corn mixture on crust. Sprinkle with ½ of cheese. Spoon beef mixture over cheese. Arrange cornmeal wedges evenly on top so that each cut pizza wedge will have 1 cornmeal wedge on top. Sprinkle with remaining cheese and olives. Bake on bottom rack in 425°F (220°C) oven for about 20 minutes, or for about 10 minutes if using partially baked crust. Cuts into 8 wedges.

__1 wedge:__ 371 Calories; 13.9 g Total Fat; 722 mg Sodium; 16 g Protein; 46 g Carbohydrate; 3 g Dietary Fiber

Pictured on page 72.

Confetti Biscuit Crust

Adds interest to any pizza with red and green flecks peeking out.

All-purpose flour	**2 cups**	**500 mL**
Baking powder	**4 tsp.**	**20 mL**
Granulated sugar	**2 tsp.**	**10 mL**
Salt	**½ tsp.**	**2 mL**
Chopped green pepper	**¼ cup**	**60 mL**
Chopped red pepper	**¼ cup**	**60 mL**
Chopped green onion	**¼ cup**	**60 mL**
Parsley flakes	**1 tsp.**	**5 mL**
Cooking oil	**¼ cup**	**60 mL**
Milk	**½ cup**	**125 mL**

Measure first 8 ingredients into medium bowl. Mix well.

Add cooking oil and milk. Stir together to form soft ball. Turn out onto lightly floured surface. Knead 8 to 10 times. Roll out and press in greased 12 inch (30 cm) pizza pan, forming rim around edge.

__⅛ crust:__ 202 Calories; 7.8 g Total Fat; 188 mg Sodium; 4 g Protein; 29 g Carbohydrate; 1 g Dietary Fiber

Pictured on page 72.

Taco Pizza

Serve with green pepper strips and sour cream. The leftover beans can be frozen, or make two pizzas.

Basic Pizza Crust dough, this page (or partially baked commercial crust)	**1**	**1**
Lean ground beef	**½ lb.**	**225 g**
Chopped onion	**⅓ cup**	**75 mL**
Can of refried beans (14 oz., 398 mL)	**½**	**½**
Envelope of taco seasoning mix (1¼ oz., 35 g)	**½**	**½**
Tomato sauce	**½ cup**	**125 mL**
Cayenne pepper	**⅛ tsp.**	**0.5 mL**
Granulated sugar	**½ tsp.**	**2 mL**
Grated medium Cheddar cheese	**1½ cups**	**375 mL**

Prepare pizza dough. Roll out and press in greased 12 inch (30 cm) pizza pan, forming rim around edge.

Scramble-fry ground beef and onion in medium non-stick frying pan until beef is no longer pink and onion is soft. Drain.

Mix next 5 ingredients in small bowl. Spread on crust. Spoon beef mixture over top.

Cover with cheese. Bake on bottom rack in 425°F (220°C) oven for about 15 minutes, or for 10 minutes if using partially baked crust. Cuts into 8 wedges.

***1 wedge:** 328 Calories; 14.1 g Total Fat; 697 mg Sodium; 16 g Protein; 34 g Carbohydrate; 3 g Dietary Fiber*

Basic Pizza Crust

A crust that will work for any regular pizza.

All-purpose flour	**2 cups**	**500 mL**
Instant yeast	**1¼ tsp.**	**6 mL**
Salt	**¼ tsp.**	**1 mL**
Warm water	**⅔ cup**	**150 mL**
Cooking oil	**2 tbsp.**	**30 mL**

Food Processor Method: Put first 3 ingredients into food processor fitted with dough blade. With machine running, pour water and cooking oil through tube in lid. Process for 50 to 60 seconds. If dough seems sticky to remove, add about ½ tsp. (2 mL) flour to make it easier to handle.

Hand Method: Put first three ingredients into medium bowl. Stir well.

Add warm water and cooking oil. Mix well until dough leaves sides of bowl. Knead on lightly floured surface for 5 to 8 minutes until smooth and elastic.

To Complete: Roll out and press in greased 12 inch (30 cm) pizza pan, forming rim around edge. Or place dough in large greased bowl, turning once to grease top. Cover with tea towel. Let stand in oven with light on and door closed for about 1 hour until doubled in size. Punch dough down. Roll out and press in greased 12 inch (30 cm) pizza pan, forming rim around edge.

***⅛ crust:** 153 Calories; 3.8 g Total Fat; 86 mg Sodium; 4 g Protein; 25 g Carbohydrate; 1 g Dietary Fiber*

TACO PIZZA CRUST: Mix ½ envelope (1¼ oz., 35 g) taco seasoning mix into dry ingredients before adding wet ingredients.

MEXICAN PIZZA CON POLLO

A substantial topping that has a yummy Mexican flavor. Serve with a dish of sour cream on the side.

Basic Pizza Crust dough, page 95	1	1
Cooking oil	2 tsp.	10 mL
Chopped onion	1 cup	250 mL
Boneless, skinless chicken breast halves (about 2), cut into ½ inch (12 mm) pieces	½ lb.	225 g
Can of refried beans (14 oz., 398 mL), see Note	½	½
Picante Salsa, page 39 (or commercial)	⅔ cup	150 mL
Can of diced green chilies, with liquid	4 oz.	114 mL
Grated medium Cheddar cheese	1 cup	250 mL
Grated Monterey Jack cheese	½ cup	125 mL

Prepare pizza dough. Roll out and press in greased 12 inch (30 cm) pizza pan, forming rim around edge.

Heat cooking oil in medium frying pan. Add onion and chicken. Sauté until onion is soft and chicken is no longer pink.

Spread refried beans on crust. Drizzle salsa over beans.

Stir green chilies with liquid into chicken mixture. Spread on salsa.

Sprinkle with Cheddar cheese, then with Monterey Jack cheese. Bake on bottom rack in 425°F (220°C) oven for 18 to 20 minutes. Cuts into 8 wedges.

1 wedge: 341 Calories; 13 g Total Fat; 852 mg Sodium; 18 g Protein; 38 g Carbohydrate; 4 g Dietary Fiber

Note: Unused refried beans can be frozen for later use, or, better yet, make 2 pizzas.

MEXICAN LASAGNE

No need to cook the noodles ahead of time.

Lean ground beef	1 lb.	454 g
Medium onion, chopped	1	1
Garlic clove, minced	1	1
Chopped fresh cilantro (or ½ tsp., 2 mL, ground coriander)	¼ cup	60 mL
Salsa	3 cups	750 mL
Chili powder	1 tsp.	5 mL
Can of tomato sauce	7½ oz.	213 mL
Water	1 cup	250 mL
Part-skim ricotta cheese	16 oz.	500 g
Large egg	1	1
Salt	½ tsp.	2 mL
Pepper	¼ tsp.	1 mL
Lasagna noodles, uncooked	12	12
Grated Monterey Jack cheese	2½ cups	625 mL

Scramble-fry ground beef in large non-stick frying pan for 5 minutes. Add onion, garlic and cilantro. Sauté until beef is no longer pink and onion is soft. Drain.

Add salsa, chili powder, tomato sauce and water. Heat and stir until boiling.

Combine ricotta cheese, egg, salt and pepper in medium bowl.

Lightly spray 9 x 13 inch (22 x 33 cm) baking dish with no-stick cooking spray. Spread 1¼ cups (300 mL) salsa mixture evenly in bottom. Cover with 4 lasagna noodles. Pour another 1¼ cups (300 mL) salsa mixture over. Add layer of 4 noodles. Spread on ricotta mixture. Add remaining 4 noodles. Pour remaining salsa mixture over all. Sprinkle with Monterey Jack cheese. Cover pan tightly with foil that has been sprayed with no-stick cooking spray. Bake in 350°F (175°C) oven for 1¼ hours. Remove foil. Bake for 15 minutes. Let stand for 10 minutes before cutting. Serves 8.

1 serving: 479 Calories; 22.3 g Total Fat; 684 mg Sodium; 33 g Protein; 37 g Carbohydrate; 3 g Dietary Fiber

MEXICAN LASAGNE

Try a different flavor. This has a good mild green chili taste.

Lasagna noodles	10-12	10-12
Boiling water	4 qts.	4 L
Cooking oil (optional)	1 tbsp.	15 mL
Salt	1 tbsp.	15 mL

MEAT SAUCE

Lean ground beef	1½ lbs.	680 g
Cooking oil	1 tbsp.	15 mL
Can of tomatoes, mashed	14 oz.	398 mL
Can of tomato paste	5½ oz.	156 mL
Granulated sugar	2-3 tsp.	10-15 mL
Salt	1½ tsp.	7 mL
Pepper	¼ tsp.	1 mL
Garlic powder	¼ tsp.	1 mL

CHEESE SAUCE

Cream cheese, softened	4 oz.	125 g
Sour cream	½ cup	125 mL
Creamed cottage cheese	1 cup	250 mL
Can of diced green chilies, drained	4 oz.	114 mL
Grated Parmesan cheese	⅓ cup	75 mL
Large egg	1	1
Chopped green onion	2 tbsp.	30 mL
Grated Monterey Jack cheese	2 cups	500 mL

Cook noodles in boiling water, cooking oil and salt in large uncovered pot or Dutch oven 14 to 16 minutes until tender but firm. Drain.

Meat Sauce: Scramble-fry ground beef in cooking oil in large saucepan until no pink remains. Drain.

Add tomato, tomato paste, sugar, salt, pepper and garlic powder. Stir. Bring to a boil. Reduce heat. Simmer, uncovered, for 20 minutes, stirring occasionally.

Cheese Sauce: Beat cream cheese and sour cream in large bowl until smooth. Add cottage cheese, green chilies, Parmesan cheese, egg and green onion. Stir.

To assemble, layer as follows in greased 9 x 13 inch (22 x 33 cm) baking dish:

1. ½ of noodles
2. ½ of meat sauce
3. Cheese sauce
4. ½ of noodles
5. ½ of meat sauce
6. Monterey Jack cheese

Cover with greased foil. Bake in 350°F (175°C) oven for 45 to 55 minutes. To brown cheese, remove foil halfway through. Let stand for 10 minutes before cutting. Cuts into 12 pieces. Serves 8.

1 piece: 513 Calories; 28.4 g Total Fat; 1163 mg Sodium; 35 g Protein; 29 g Carbohydrate; 2 g Dietary Fiber

CHICKEN ENCHILADAS

This begins with a filling and ends with a pan full of wonderful enchiladas.

Cooking oil	2 tbsp.	30 mL
Boneless, skinless, chicken breast halves (about 4), diced	1 lb.	454 g
Chopped onion	1 cup	250 mL
Garlic clove, minced (or ¼ tsp., 1 mL, garlic powder)	1	1
Can of sliced mushrooms, drained	10 oz.	284 mL
Can of diced green chilies, drained	4 oz.	114 mL
Sour cream	1 cup	250 mL
Chili powder	1 tsp.	5 mL
Ground cumin	1 tsp.	5 mL
Salt	½ tsp.	2 mL
Pepper	¼ tsp.	1 mL
Cooking oil	½ cup	125 mL
Corn tortillas (6 inch, 15 cm, size)	16	16
Grated medium Cheddar (or Monterey Jack) cheese	2 cups	500 mL

TOPPING

Sour cream	2 cups	500 mL
Grated medium Cheddar (or Monterey Jack) cheese	2 cups	500 mL

Heat cooking oil in frying pan. Add chicken, onion and garlic. Stir-fry until chicken is no longer pink.

Stir next 7 ingredients together well in medium bowl. Add chicken mixture.

Heat second amount of cooking oil in frying pan. Using tongs, dip each tortilla into cooking oil to soften for 3 to 5 seconds per side. Add more cooking oil if needed. Remove with slotted spoon to paper towels to drain. Place scant ¼ cup (60 mL) chicken mixture in center of each tortilla.

Add 2 tbsp. (30 mL) cheese. Roll tortilla tightly around filling. Arrange seam side down in 1 or 2 greased baking pans. Bake, uncovered, in 350°F (175°C) oven for 15 minutes until hot.

Topping: Spread sour cream on top. Sprinkle with cheese. Bake for about 5 minutes until cheese is melted. Makes 16 enchiladas.

2 enchiladas: 829 Calories; 50.1 g Total Fat; 2003 mg Sodium; 48 g Protein; 49 g Carbohydrate; 5 g Dietary Fiber

Pictured on page 36.

When cutting raw chicken, use a plastic cutting board instead of wood. Plastic is easier to clean since it doesn't absorb liquid.

★★★★★★★★★★★★★★★★★★★★★★★★★★★★★★★★★★

CORNY BEEF ENCHILADAS

You can make these as spicy as you like by adjusting the kind of salsa you use as well as adding jalapeño peppers.

Chopped cooked roast beef	2 cups	500 mL
Frozen kernel corn, thawed	1 cup	250 mL
Can of diced green chilies, drained	4 oz.	114 mL
Salsa	⅔ cup	150 mL
Ground cumin	½ tsp.	2 mL
Salt	½ tsp.	2 mL
Salsa	⅔ cup	150 mL
Corn tortillas (6 inch, 15 cm, size)	8	8
Salsa	⅔ cup	150 mL
Grated sharp Cheddar cheese	1 cup	250 mL
sliced pitted ripe olives (optional)	2 tbsp.	30 mL
Sliced jalapeño pepper (optional)	2 tbsp.	30 mL

Combine first 6 ingredients in medium bowl.

Spread second amount of salsa in greased casserole or baking dish large enough to hold 8 enchiladas in single layer.

Place 1 tortilla on working surface. Cover remaining tortillas with damp tea towel to keep from drying out. Place about ⅓ cup (75 mL) beef mixture on tortilla. Fold sides over center. Lay, folded side up, on salsa in casserole. Repeat with remaining tortillas.

Drizzle third amount of salsa over enchiladas. Sprinkle with cheese, olives and jalapeño pepper. Cover. Bake in 350°F (175°C) oven for 45 minutes. Remove cover. Bake for about 15 minutes until very hot. Makes 8 enchiladas.

2 enchiladas: 529 Calories; 16.7 g Total Fat; 2665 mg Sodium; 38 g Protein; 62 g Carbohydrate; 6 g Dietary Fiber

Pictured on page 53 and on back cover.

LAZY CHICKEN ENCHILADAS

Cooked in casserole. Get the flavor without all the individual rolling.

Skinless bone-in chicken parts	3 lbs.	1.4 kg
Water, to cover		
Margarine (or butter)	1 tsp.	5 mL
Chopped onion	1 cup	250 mL
Can of condensed cream of mushroom soup	10 oz.	284 mL
Can of condensed cream of chicken soup	10 oz.	284 mL
Can of diced green chilies, drained	4 oz.	114 mL
Corn tortillas (6 inch, 15 cm, size)	9	9
Grated medium Cheddar cheese	1 cup	250 mL

Put chicken and water in large saucepan. Cover. Bring to a boil. Cook for 45 to 60 minutes until tender. Cool chicken in broth. When cool, remove chicken. Remove chicken from bone. Shred or chop chicken. Reserve ½ cup (125 mL) broth. Discard remaining broth.

Heat margarine in frying pan. Add onion. Sauté until soft.

Combine next 3 ingredients in large bowl. Add reserved chicken broth. Stir. Add chicken and onion. Stir.

Layer ⅓ of chicken mixture in ungreased 3 quart (3 L) casserole. Cover with 3 tortillas. Repeat 2 more times. Sprinkle cheese over all. Cover. Bake in 350°F (175°C) oven for about 30 minutes. Remove cover. Bake for about 10 minutes until hot and bubbly. Serves 6.

1 serving: 465 Calories; 19.5 g Total Fat; 1129 mg Sodium; 36 g Protein; 37 g Carbohydrate; 3 g Dietary Fiber

CRAB ENCHILADAS

Heat up this Mexican-style dish by using canned jalepeño peppers instead of the chilies. The sauce can be prepared ahead and reheated when ready to assemble.

Margarine (or butter)	1 tbsp.	15 mL
Chopped onion	1 cup	250 mL
Can of diced tomatoes, with juice	14 oz.	398 mL
Can of tomato sauce	7½ oz.	213 mL
Can of diced green chilies, drained	4 oz.	114 mL
Granulated sugar	1 tsp.	5 mL
Dried whole oregano	½ tsp.	2 mL
Dried sweet basil	¼ tsp.	1 mL
Salt	¼ tsp.	1 mL
Seasoned salt	⅛ tsp.	0.5 mL
Crabmeat, cartilage removed (or imitation crabmeat)	1 lb.	454 g
Grated Monterey Jack cheese	½ cup	125 mL
Can of pitted ripe olives, chopped	4½ oz.	125 mL
Corn tortillas (6 inch, 15 cm, size)	12	12
Grated Monterey Jack cheese	1 cup	250 mL

Melt margarine in frying pan. Add onion. Sauté until onion is soft.

Combine next 8 ingredients in medium saucepan. Mix well. Add onion. Bring to a boil, stirring often. Reduce heat. Simmer, uncovered, for 10 minutes. Cover bottom of ungreased 9 x 13 inch (22 x 33 cm) baking dish with ¼ cup (60 mL) sauce. Set aside. Reserve ½ cup (125 mL) sauce.

Stir crabmeat, first amount of cheese, reserved sauce and olives together in small bowl.

Dip tortillas quickly, 1 at a time, into remaining sauce. Place ¼ cup (60 mL) crab mixture at 1 end of tortilla. Roll up. Place, seam side down, in prepared pan. Spoon remaining sauce over rolls.

Scatter second amount of cheese over all. Bake, uncovered, in 350°F (175°C) oven for about 25 minutes until heated through. Makes 12 enchiladas.

2 enchiladas: 410 Calories; 14.7 g Total Fat; 1272 mg Sodium; 27 g Protein; 44 g Carbohydrate; 5 g Dietary Fiber

ENCHILADAS

A meatless variety.

Margarine (or butter)	2 tbsp.	30 mL
Large onion, chopped	1	1
Cooking oil	1 tbsp.	15 mL
Flour tortillas (8 inch, 20 cm, size)	6	6
Chili sauce	1 cup	250 mL
Grated Monterey Jack cheese	2 cups	500 mL
Grated Cheddar cheese	1 cup	250 mL

Melt margarine in frying pan. Add onion. Sauté until soft.

Heat cooking oil in separate frying pan. Dip tortillas, one at a time, into cooking oil to soften. Dip into chili sauce.

Divide ½ of Monterey Jack cheese, ½ of Cheddar cheese and ½ of onion among tortillas. Roll up. Place close together in pan. Pour remaining chili sauce over all. Sprinkle remaining cheeses and onion over top. Cover. Bake in 350°F (175°C) oven for 20 minutes. Makes 6 enchiladas.

1 enchilada: 453 Calories; 25.6 g Total Fat; 1163 mg Sodium; 20 g Protein; 36 g Carbohydrate; 3 g Dietary Fiber

HAMBURGER ENCHILADA: Add ½ to 1 pound (225 to 454 g) ground beef to onion in frying pan. Scramble-fry until onion is soft and beef is no longer pink.

CHICKEN ENCHILADAS

Shredded chicken combined with cheese and rolled into bundles then topped and baked with a tomato and green chili sauce. Allow extra time to prepare. To be authentic use Monterey Jack cheese. Serve with sour cream and green onion.

Bone-in chicken breasts (about 2)	1½ lbs.	680 g
Bone-in chicken thighs (about 6)	1¾ lbs.	790 g
Chopped onion	½ cup	125 mL
Sliced celery	¼ cup	60 mL
Bay leaf	1	1
Salt	2 tsp.	10 mL
Pepper	½ tsp.	2 mL
Water, to cover		
FILLING		
Margarine (or butter)	2 tbsp.	30 mL
Chopped onion	1 cup	250 mL
Grated Monterey Jack cheese	1½ cups	375 mL
Grated Parmesan cheese	⅓ cup	75 mL
Cooking oil	½ cup	125 mL
Corn tortillas (6 inch, 15 cm, size)	16	16
SAUCE		
Can of condensed cream of chicken soup	10 oz.	284 mL
Can of diced tomatoes, drained	28 oz.	796 mL
Cans of diced green chilies (4 oz., 114 mL, each)	2	2
Sour cream	½ cup	125 mL
Granulated sugar	1 tsp.	5 mL
Garlic powder	¼ tsp.	1 mL
Onion powder	¼ tsp.	1 mL
Grated medium Cheddar cheese	2 cups	500 mL

Combine first 8 ingredients in large uncovered pot or Dutch oven. Boil for 30 to 40 minutes until chicken is tender. Cool chicken in broth. Drain. Reserve 2 cups (500 mL) broth. Remove chicken from bones. Shred chicken. Should have about 4 cups (1 L) chicken.

Filling: Melt margarine in frying pan. Add onion. Sauté until soft. Cool.

Measure Monterey Jack cheese and Parmesan cheese into medium bowl. Add onion and chicken. Toss to mix.

Heat cooking oil in frying pan. Using tongs, dip tortillas, one at a time, into oil for 3 to 5 seconds per side to soften, adding more cooking oil if needed. Remove with slotted spoon to paper towels to drain. Place scant ¼ cup (60 mL) chicken mixture on tortilla. Press filling together. Roll tortilla tightly around chicken. Place in 1 or 2 greased pans in single layer, seam side down.

Sauce: Mix first 7 ingredients together in medium bowl. Pour over enchiladas.

Sprinkle Cheddar cheese over top. Bake in 350°F (175°C) oven for about 25 minutes until bubbly hot. Makes 16 enchiladas.

2 enchiladas: 432 Calories; 27.5 g Total Fat; 438 mg Sodium; 26 g Protein; 21 g Carbohydrate; 2 g Dietary Fiber

ACAPULCO BEEF FILET

Have two skillets going at once to save time.

Large onion, cut lengthwise into slivers	1	1
Margarine (or butter)	1 tbsp.	15 mL
Medium red pepper, cut into 1½ inch (3.8 cm) chunks	1	1
Medium yellow pepper, cut into 1½ inch (3.8 cm) chunks	1	1
Chili sauce	3 tbsp.	50 mL
Condensed beef broth	½ cup	125 mL
Salt	½ tsp.	2 mL
Freshly ground pepper	1 tsp.	5 mL
Beef filet (or tenderloin) steaks (4 oz., 125 g, each)	4	4
Freshly ground pepper, to taste		
Cooking oil	1 tbsp.	15 mL
Tequila	2 tbsp.	30 mL
Lime juice	1 tbsp.	15 mL
Salt	¼ tsp.	1 mL

Sauté onion in margarine in non-stick frying pan until onion is golden. Add peppers. Sauté for 2 to 3 minutes. Add chili sauce, beef broth, salt and pepper. Cover. Simmer for 7 minutes. Drain.

Blot steaks with paper towel. Season with pepper. Rub in well.

Heat cooking oil in cast-iron frying pan until very hot. Sear steaks for 3 to 4 minutes per side or to desired doneness.

Arrange onion mixture on warmed platter. Place steaks on top. Add tequila and lime juice to frying pan. Simmer for 2 to 3 minutes. Sprinkle with salt. Pour over steaks.

1 serving: 271 Calories; 13.7 g Total Fat; 768 mg Sodium; 25 g Protein; 7 g Carbohydrate; 1 g Dietary Fiber

MEXICAN CHORIZO

A tasty, easy-to-make sausage meat.

Ground pork	3 lbs.	1.4 kg
White vinegar	⅓ cup	75 mL
Chili powder	2 tbsp.	30 mL
Salt	1 tbsp.	15 mL
Pepper	½ tsp.	2 mL
Dried whole oregano	2 tsp.	10 mL
Garlic powder	½ tsp.	2 mL

Put ground pork into large bowl.

Combine remaining 6 ingredients in separate small bowl. Mix well, adding water if too dry. Add to pork. Mix thoroughly. Cover. Chill at least 1 day to allow flavors to blend. Divide into 4 equal balls. Divide each ball into 4 patties. Fry, browning both sides, until sausage is no longer pink. Makes 16 patties.

2 patties: 238 Calories; 8.9 g Total Fat; 1003 mg Sodium; 36 g Protein; 2 g Carbohydrate; 1 g Dietary Fiber

Mexican

Side Dishes

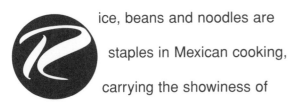

ice, beans and noodles are staples in Mexican cooking, carrying the showiness of pimentos, chilies, and other vegetables and spices. Add Tamale Rice Dish, page 103, or Noodles Con Queso, page 110, to dinner to punch up your main course. For a twist, Mexican Carrots, page 109, teams up with cream cheese and chilies while portobello mushrooms star in Sante Fe Mushroom, page 104.

TAMALE RICE DISH

This has the popular taco seasoning with a touch of chili powder which may easily be increased.

Lean ground beef	1 lb.	454 g
Finely chopped onion	1 cup	250 mL
Chopped green pepper	1 cup	250 mL
Garlic salt	1 tsp.	5 mL
Pepper	⅛ tsp.	0.5 mL
Cans of stewed tomatoes, 2 with juice, broken up (14 oz., 398 mL, each)		2
Can of kernel corn, with liquid	12 oz.	341 mL
Envelope of taco seasoning mix	1¼ oz.	35 g
Granulated sugar	1 tsp.	5 mL
Chili powder (or more, to taste)	½ tsp.	2 mL
Water	½ cup	125 mL
Long grain white rice, uncooked	⅔ cup	150 mL
Grated medium Cheddar cheese	½ cup	125 mL
Light sour cream	¾ cup	175 mL
Sliced pitted ripe olives	¼ cup	60 mL
Corn chips, for garnish	1 cup	250 mL

Scramble-fry first 5 ingredients in large non-stick frying pan until onion is soft and beef is no longer pink. Drain.

Stir in next 7 ingredients. Cover. Simmer for about 20 minutes, stirring occasionally, until rice is tender and liquid is absorbed. Turn into serving dish.

Sprinkle with cheese. Dab sour cream over top. Sprinkle with olives. Garnish with corn chips. Serves 4.

1 serving: 566 Calories; 19.6 g Total Fat; 2289 mg Sodium; 33 g Protein; 69 g Carbohydrate; 6 g Dietary Fiber

SIMPLE RICE

A variation of rice that is much used and enjoyed.

Long grain white rice	2 cups	500 mL
Hot water, to cover		
Cooking oil	¼ cup	60 mL
Medium tomatoes	2	2
Chopped onion	½ cup	125 mL
Water	4 cups	1 L
Salt	1 tsp.	5 mL
Chicken bouillon powder	2 tsp.	10 mL

Cover rice in bowl with hot water. Let stand for 15 minutes. Drain. Cover with cold water. Drain. Continue to rinse with cold water until water runs clear when draining.

Sauté rice in cooking oil in frying pan for about 10 minutes until rice is golden.

Combine remaining 5 ingredients in blender. Process until smooth. Pour into medium saucepan. Heat through. Add rice. It will spatter quite a bit. Bring to a boil. Reduce heat. Cover. Simmer slowly for about 15 minutes until water is absorbed. Fluff with fork. Serves 8.

1 serving: 255 Calories; 7.8 g Total Fat; 507 mg Sodium; 4 g Protein; 42 g Carbohydrate; 1 g Dietary Fiber

SANTA FE MUSHROOM

This recipe easily multiplies to your number of guests. There's plenty of room on the barbecue for more.

Salsa	⅓ cup	75 mL
Garlic clove, minced	1	1
Chili powder	½ tsp.	2 mL
Ground cumin	¼ tsp.	1 mL
Large portobello mushroom, nicely shaped	1	1
Cooking oil	1 tsp.	5 mL
Lettuce leaves (optional)	1-2	1-2

Combine first 4 ingredients in blender. Process until smooth. Makes ⅓ cup (75 mL) marinade.

Remove stem from mushroom. Scrape and discard black "gills" from around underside of mushroom with spoon. Pour marinade over mushroom. Let stand at room temperature for 30 minutes, turning several times.

Preheat barbecue to medium-high. Remove mushroom, reserving marinade for basting. Brush mushroom inside and out with cooking oil. Cook on greased grill for 5 to 6 minutes, turning and basting surface with marinade several times, until tender. Discard any remaining marinade.

Slice mushroom and serve on a bed of lettuce leaves. Serves 1.

1 serving: 134 Calories; 5.6 g Total Fat; 1312 mg Sodium; 5 g Protein; 20 g Carbohydrate; 4 g Dietary Fiber

Pictured on page 90.

SPAGHETTI

Served in Mexico often as an alternative to rice. This has a smooth red pepper sauce and melting chunks of cheese. Heat in the oven.

Spaghetti	1 lb.	454 g
Boiling water	5 qts.	5 L
Cooking oil	2 tbsp.	30 mL
Salt	4 tsp.	20 mL
Light cream	1 cup	250 mL
Large red pepper, cut up	1	1
Diced Monterey Jack cheese	2 cups	500 mL

Cook spaghetti in boiling water, cooking oil and salt in large uncovered pot or Dutch oven for 11 to 13 minutes until tender but firm. Drain. Return spaghetti to pot.

Put cream and red pepper into blender. Process until smooth. Pour into small saucepan. Heat, but don't boil. Pour over spaghetti.

Add cheese. Toss to coat. Turn into greased 3 quart (3 L) casserole. Cover with foil. Bake in 350°F (175°C) oven for about 25 minutes until bubbling hot. Serves 8.

1 serving: 362 Calories; 13.2 g Total Fat; 177 mg Sodium; 16 g Protein; 45 g Carbohydrate; 2 g Dietary Fiber

GREEN RICE

Delicate color adds a nice variation to meals.

Long grain white rice	2 cups	500 mL
Hot water, to cover		
Large green peppers, cut up	3	3
Chopped onion	1 cup	250 mL
Parsley flakes	⅓ cup	75 mL
Garlic clove	1	1
Chicken bouillon cubes, (⅕ oz., 6 g, each)	4	4
Water	1 cup	250 mL
Salt	1 tsp.	5 mL
Pepper	⅛ tsp.	0.5 mL
Cooking oil	3 tbsp.	50 mL
Water	3 cups	750 mL

Cover rice in bowl with very hot water. Let stand for 15 minutes. Drain. Cover with cold water. Drain. Continue to rinse with cold water until water runs clear when draining.

Measure next 8 ingredients into blender. Process until smooth. Set aside.

Put cooking oil into large saucepan. Add rice. Stir-fry on medium until rice is golden. Add contents of blender.

Add remaining water. Bring to a boil. Reduce heat. Cover. Simmer for about 15 minutes until tender and liquid is absorbed. Fluff with fork. Serves 8.

1 serving: 249 Calories; 5.8 g Total Fat; 1055 mg Sodium; 5 g Protein; 44 g Carbohydrate; 1 g Dietary Fiber

Pictured on page 89.

CALABACITAS

This cah-lah-bah-SEE-tahs contains zucchini, corn, tomato sauce and onion. The word means "little squash."

Chopped onion	1 cup	250 mL
Garlic clove, minced	1	1
Cooking oil	2 tbsp.	30 mL
Zucchini (about 6 inches, 15 cm, long), with peel, sliced	4-5	4-5
Kernel corn, fresh or frozen	1½ cups	375 mL
Can of tomato sauce	7½ oz.	213 mL
Can of diced green chilies, drained	4 oz.	114 mL
Granulated sugar	½ tsp.	2 mL
Salt	1 tsp.	5 mL
Pepper	⅛ tsp.	0.5 mL
Grated Monterey Jack cheese	½ cup	125 mL

Sauté onion and garlic in cooking oil in frying pan for about 3 minutes until onion is soft.

Add zucchini and corn. Heat and stir for 3 or 4 minutes until tender.

Add next 5 ingredients. Bring to a boil. Pour into large bowl.

Sprinkle with cheese. Serves 8.

1 serving: 117 Calories; 6.2 g Total Fat; 646 mg Sodium; 4 g Protein; 14 g Carbohydrate; 3 g Dietary Fiber

Pictured on page 89.

To prevent sticky rice, avoid stirring while rice is cooking.

TAMALE PIE

A bright yellow topping over a dark reddish filling.

Chopped onion	1 cup	250 mL
Chopped green pepper	½ cup	125 mL
Garlic clove, minced (or ¼ tsp., 1 mL, garlic powder)	1	1
Cooking oil	1 tbsp.	15 mL
Can of diced tomatoes, with juice	14 oz.	398 mL
Can of Romano beans, drained, rinsed and mashed	19 oz.	540 mL
Bulgur	⅔ cup	150 mL
Ketchup	2 tbsp.	30 mL
Chili powder	1 tbsp.	15 mL
Salt	1 tsp.	5 mL
Pepper	¼ tsp.	1 mL
CRUST		
Yellow cornmeal	1 cup	250 mL
Baking powder	1 tsp.	5 mL
Salt	½ tsp.	2 mL
Large egg, fork-beaten	1	1
Milk	¾ cup	175 mL
Cooking oil	2 tbsp.	30 mL

Sauté onion, green pepper and garlic in cooking oil in frying pan until soft.

Add next 7 ingredients. Heat and stir until boiling. Reduce heat. Cover. Simmer for about 15 minutes, stirring often to keep from burning. Mixture will be quite thick. Turn into ungreased 8 x 8 inch (20 x 20 cm) baking dish. Set aside.

Crust: Stir cornmeal, baking powder and salt together in small bowl. Add egg, milk and cooking oil. Stir. Pour over tomato mixture. Bake, uncovered, in 350°F (175°C) oven for about 35 minutes until firm. Serves 6.

1 serving: 336 Calories; 10.2 g Total Fat; 913 mg Sodium; 12 g Protein; 53 g Carbohydrate; 13 g Dietary Fiber

BEANS MOLE

A rich, deep color and flavor. Serve as a tasty side dish for ribs, roast or other meats.

Hard margarine (butter browns too fast)	1 tsp.	5 mL
Chopped onion	¼ cup	60 mL
Can of beans in tomato sauce	14 oz.	398 mL
Brown sugar, packed	1 tbsp.	15 mL
Fancy (mild) molasses	1 tsp.	5 mL
Ketchup	¼ cup	60 mL
Worcestershire sauce	½ tsp.	2 mL
Cocoa, sifted if lumpy	1 tbsp.	15 mL

Melt margarine in large saucepan. Add onion. Sauté until golden.

Add remaining 6 ingredients. Turn into ungreased 1 quart (1 L) casserole. Bake, uncovered, in 350°F (175°C) oven for about 35 minutes until hot and browning around outside edges. Makes 2 cups (500 mL).

½ cup (125 mL): 151 Calories; 1.7 g Total Fat; 659 mg Sodium; 6 g Protein; 33 g Carbohydrate; 9 g Dietary Fiber

1. Caramel Flan, page 115
2. Mango Fluff, page 113
3. Rice Pudding, page 113

SUMMER SQUASH

Parmesan cheese, green chilies and onion add flavor to zucchini.

Chopped onion	1 cup	250 mL
Cooking oil	¼ cup	60 mL
Medium zucchini (or yellow squash)	6	6
Can of diced green chilies, drained	4 oz.	114 mL
Milk	⅓ cup	75 mL
Salt	½ tsp.	2 mL
Pepper	¼ tsp.	1 mL
Grated Parmesan cheese	⅓ cup	75 mL

Sauté onion in cooking oil in frying pan for 3 to 4 minutes.

Add zucchini. Cook for about 5 minutes until tender.

Add green chilies, milk, salt and pepper. Heat through. Turn into serving bowl.

Sprinkle with Parmesan. Toss to mix. Serves 8.

1 serving: 114 Calories; 8.9 g Total Fat; 357 mg Sodium; 4 g Protein; 6 g Carbohydrate; 2 g Dietary Fiber

MEXICAN CARROTS

Nippy and creamy, these are excellent. Garnish with parsley sprigs for company.

Diced or sliced carrot	3 cups	750 mL
Salted water		
Cream cheese	4 oz.	125 g
Can of diced green chilies, drained	4 oz.	114 mL
Milk	¼ cup	60 mL
Salt	½ tsp.	2 mL
Pepper	⅛ tsp.	0.5 mL

Cook carrot in salted water until tender. Drain.

Cut in cream cheese. Add green chilies, milk, salt and pepper. Heat and stir until melted and heated through. Pour into serving bowl.

Serves 4.

1 serving: 158 Calories; 11.3 g Total Fat; 662 mg Sodium; 4 g Protein; 11 g Carbohydrate; 2 g Dietary Fiber

GREEN BEANS AND TOMATOES

Colorful, good and so easy to prepare.

Bacon slices, diced	6	6
Chopped onion	1 cup	250 mL
Can of diced tomatoes, drained	14 oz.	398 mL
Cans of cut green beans (14 oz., 398 mL, each), drained	2	2

Sauté bacon and onion in frying pan until cooked. Drain.

Heat tomatoes and green beans in medium saucepan. Add bacon and onion. Serves 8.

1 serving: 50 Calories; 2.5 g Total Fat; 187 mg Sodium; 2 g Protein; 5 g Carbohydrate; 2 g Dietary Fiber

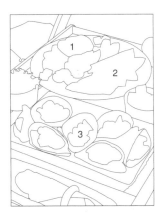

1. Margaritagrill, page 112
2. Fresh Fruit Quesadillas, page 114
3. Fruity Burritos, page 114

REFRIED BEANS

Pinto beans make the lightest-colored product followed by red beans and then black beans. A must for a Mexican meal.

Bacon slices, diced	6	6
Dried pinto (or red or black) beans	2 cups	500 mL
Hot water, to cover		
Chopped onion	1 cup	250 mL
Bay leaf	1	1
Salt	1 tsp.	5 mL
Garlic powder	¼ tsp.	1 mL

Pepper, sprinkle (optional)
Grated Monterey Jack cheese, to garnish

Cook bacon in frying pan until no longer pink. Remove with slotted spoon to paper towels to drain. Reserve ¼ cup (60 mL) drippings.

Measure next 6 ingredients into large heavy saucepan. Add bacon. Bring to a boil. Cover. Reduce heat. Simmer for about 1 hour 45 minutes until tender. If too thick, add more water. Discard bay leaf. Mash, leaving up to ¼ of mixture coarsely mashed.

Put reserved bacon drippings into frying pan. Add bean mixture. Heat, stirring often. Sprinkle with pepper and grated cheese. Makes about 5 cups (1.25 L).

1 cup (250 mL): 276 Calories; 10.4 g Total Fat; 469 mg Sodium; 12 g Protein; 34 g Carbohydrate; 5 g Dietary Fiber

Variation: Stir about ¾ cup (175 mL) grated Monterey Jack cheese into hot bean mixture before serving.

NOODLES CON QUESO

A different and very tasty pot of noodles. The red and green bits in a creamy sauce make noodles kahn-KAY-soh very colorful.

Finely chopped green pepper	2 tbsp.	30 mL
Process cheese loaf (such as Velveeta)	8 oz.	250 g
Light cream	½ cup	125 mL
Can of diced green chilies, drained	4 oz.	114 mL
Chopped pimiento	2 tsp.	10 mL
Paprika	¼ tsp.	1 mL
Broad egg noodles	1 lb.	454 g
Boiling water	4 qts.	4 L
Cooking oil (optional)	1 tbsp.	15 mL
Salt	1 tbsp.	15 mL

Cook pepper in small amount of water in medium saucepan until tender-crisp. Drain off water.

Add next 5 ingredients. Heat on low until cheese is melted. Makes 1⅓ cups (325 mL) sauce.

Cook noodles in boiling water, cooking oil and salt in large uncovered pot or Dutch oven for 5 to 7 minutes until tender but firm. Drain. Add to sauce. Toss well. Makes 7 cups (1.75 L).

1 cup (250 mL): 390 Calories; 13.4 g Total Fat; 701 mg Sodium; 17 g Protein; 50 g Carbohydrate; 2 g Dietary Fiber

Pictured on page 90.

★★★★★★★★★★★★★★★★★★★★★★★★★★★★★★★★★

SPANISH LENTIL PILAF

Slightly spicy with a chunky look. Very good.

Can of stewed tomatoes, with juice	14 oz.	398 mL
Water	2 cups	500 mL
Brown rice, uncooked	½ cup	125 mL
Green lentils	¼ cup	60 mL
Red lentils	¼ cup	60 mL
Chopped onion	½ cup	125 mL
Chopped celery	¼ cup	60 mL
Instant vegetable stock mix	1 tbsp.	15 mL
Dried sweet basil	1½ tsp.	7 mL
Pepper	¼ tsp.	1 mL
Grated medium or sharp Cheddar cheese	14 oz.	398 mL

Measure first 10 ingredients into saucepan. Bring to a boil, stirring often. Cover. Reduce heat. Simmer for about 1 hour until rice and lentils are tender.

Add cheese. Stir until melted. Makes 3½ cups (875 mL).

½ cup (125 mL): 198 Calories; 6.4 g Total Fat; 412 mg Sodium; 10 g Protein; 26 g Carbohydrate; 3 g Dietary Fiber

SPANISH RICE

Be sure to try this, especially if you have never tried tomatoes with rice.

Long grain white rice, uncooked	1 cup	250 mL
Can of condensed onion soup	10 oz.	284 mL
Can of sliced mushrooms, drained (optional)	10 oz.	284 mL
Water	1¼ cups	300 mL
Margarine (or butter)	¼ cup	60 mL
Can of diced tomatoes, drained	1 cup	250 mL

Combine first 5 ingredients in saucepan. Bring to a boil. Cover. Reduce heat. Simmer for about 25 minutes until rice is tender and water is absorbed.

Add tomatoes. Heat through. Serves 4.

1 serving: 333 Calories; 13.8 g Total Fat; 866 mg Sodium; 6 g Protein; 47 g Carbohydrate; 2 g Dietary Fiber

Desserts

Say adios to mealtime with one of these luscious finales. Mexican cooks turn to local fruit for their inspiration, such as Mango Fluff, page 113, or Fresh Fruit Quesadilla, page 114. The Caramel Flan and Sopaipillas, both on page 115, are traditional Spanish-inspired desserts your guests will savor with a cup of tea or coffee.

MARGARITAGRILL

Do this with friends sitting around a table on the deck or patio. Serve with cheese on the side.

Tequila	¼ cup	60 mL
Orange-flavored liqueur (such asTriple Sec or Grand Marnier)	¼ cup	60 mL
Freshly squeezed lemon juice	1 tbsp.	15 mL
Finely grated lemon peel	1 tsp.	5 mL
Freshly squeezed lime juice	1 tbsp.	15 mL
Finely grated lime peel	1 tsp.	5 mL
Brown sugar, packed	¼ cup	60 mL
Slightly green bananas, peeled and cut into slices on diagonal	2	2
Medium apple, cored and sliced into rings	1	1
Large orange, peeled and sliced crosswise	1	1
Medium nectarines (or peaches), stones removed, cut into 6 wedges each	2	2

Preheat lightly sprayed electric grill to high. Stir first 7 ingredients together in small bowl until brown sugar is dissolved. Makes ¾ cup (175 mL) marinade.

Toss all 4 fruits with marinade in large bowl. Let stand at room temperature for 30 minutes. Drain and discard marinade. Cook fruit on grill for about 1 minute per side. Serves 6.

1 serving: 132 Calories; 0.5 g Total Fat; 2 mg Sodium; 1 g Protein; 28 g Carbohydrate; 2 g Dietary Fiber

Pictured on page 108.

RICE PUDDING

This just might be the best rice pudding you will ever eat.

Long grain white rice, uncooked	1 cup	250 mL
Water	2 cups	500 mL
Cinnamon stick (about 4 inches, 10 cm)	1	1
Milk	4 cups	1 L
Granulated sugar	1 cup	250 mL
Raisins	½ cup	125 mL
Salt	¼ tsp.	1 mL
Egg yolks (large)	3	3
Vanilla	1 tsp.	5 mL

Combine rice, water and cinnamon stick in medium saucepan. Cover. Bring to a boil. Reduce heat. Simmer for about 15 minutes until rice is tender and water is absorbed. Remove cinnamon stick.

Heat milk in heavy saucepan. Stir in sugar, raisins and salt. Add rice. Simmer, uncovered, for about 15 minutes until thick but still soft, stirring often.

Beat egg yolks in small bowl. Stir in vanilla. Add about ½ cup (125 mL) hot rice to egg yolk mixture. Stir into rice. Heat and stir for about 1 minute. Serves 8.

1 serving: 297 Calories; 3.5 g Total Fat; 155 mg Sodium; 7 g Protein; 60 g Carbohydrate; 1 g Dietary Fiber

Pictured on page 107.

MANGO FLUFF

And a light bit of fluff it is. A milky peach color.

Cold water	½ cup	125 mL
Envelopes of unflavored gelatin (¼ oz., 7 g, each)	2	2
Granulated sugar	¾ cup	175 mL
Lemon juice	2 tbsp.	30 mL
Salt	⅛ tsp.	0.5 mL
Mashed mango (or papaya)	2 cups	500 mL
Rum flavoring	½ tsp.	2 mL
Vanilla	¼ tsp.	1 mL
Whipping cream (or 2 envelopes of dessert Topping, prepared)	2 cups	500 mL
Rum flavoring	¼ tsp.	1 mL
Slivered or flaked almonds, toasted	2 tbsp.	30 mL

Measure cold water into saucepan. Sprinkle gelatin over top. Let stand for 5 minutes. Heat and stir on medium until gelatin is dissolved.

Add sugar, lemon juice and salt. Heat and stir until sugar is dissolved. Remove from heat.

Add mango, first amount of rum flavoring and vanilla. Mix well. Chill until firm.

Beat cream until stiff. Reserve and chill 1 cup (250 mL). Fold remainder into thickened mango mixture. Turn into serving bowl. Chill.

Stir in second amount of rum flavoring to reserved whipped cream. Spread on top of mango mixture. Sprinkle with almonds. Serves 8.

1 serving: 314 Calories; 21.4 g Total Fat; 70 mg Sodium; 3 g Protein; 30 g Carbohydrate; 1 g Dietary Fiber

Pictured on page 107.

FRESH FRUIT QUESADILLAS

Almost like a Danish pastry, without all the calories! Creamy texture inside.

Light cream cheese, softened	**4 oz.**	**125 g**
Brown sugar, packed	**2 tbsp.**	**30 mL**
Vanilla	**½ tsp.**	**2 mL**
Flour tortillas (10 inch, 25 cm, size)	**4**	**4**
Finely diced apple, with peel	**1 cup**	**250 mL**
Ground cinnamon, sprinkle		

Preheat lightly sprayed electric grill to medium-low. Combine cream cheese, brown sugar and vanilla in small bowl until smooth.

Spread mixture on 2 tortillas.

Divide apple between remaining 2 tortillas. Sprinkle with cinnamon. Cover with first 2 tortillas. Place, apple side down, on grill. Cook for 1½ to 2 minutes. Carefully turn over. Cook for 1½ to 2 minutes until crispy and browned. Let stand for 1 minute. Cuts into 4 wedges each, for a total of 8.

1 wedge: 137 Calories; 3 g Total Fat; 252 mg Sodium; 5 g Protein; 23 g Carbohydrate; trace Dietary Fiber

Pictured on page 108.

Variation: Omit apples. Use 1 cup (250 mL) mashed bananas.

FRUITY BURRITOS

So different. So pretty. Eat it out of your hand. Try all sorts of fruits and toppings.

Fresh raspberries	**⅔ cup**	**150 mL**
Fresh blueberries (or frozen, thawed)	**⅓ cup**	**75 mL**
Sliced strawberries	**⅓ cup**	**75 mL**
Low-fat creamed cottage cheese	**¼ cup**	**60 mL**
Skim milk	**4 tsp.**	**20 mL**
Lemon juice	**¾ tsp.**	**4 mL**
Liquid sweetener	**½ tsp.**	**2 mL**
Flour tortillas (6 inch, 15 cm, size), warmed (see Tip, page 85)	**8**	**8**

Combine fruit in shallow dish. Stir gently to mix.

Measure cottage cheese, milk, lemon juice and sweetener into blender. Process until smooth.

Fold warmed tortillas in half then in half again. Lift 1 side to form a hollow. Spoon about 2½ tbsp. (37 mL) or about ⅛ of fruit into hollow. Add about 1 tsp. (5 mL) cottage cheese mixture. Hold tortilla upright so mixture will run down through fruit. Repeat. Makes 8 burritos.

1 burrito: 107 Calories; trace Total Fat; 135 mg Sodium; 4 g Protein; 21 g Carbohydrate; 1 g Dietary Fiber

Pictured on page 108.

CARAMEL FLAN

A different custard with condensed milk for flavor and a yummy caramel topping. A traditional Mexican dessert.

Granulated sugar	¾ cup	175 mL
Large eggs	5	5
Can of sweetened condensed milk	11 oz.	300 mL
Can of evaporated milk	13½ oz.	385 mL
Vanilla	1 tsp.	5 mL

Caramel roses (see Note)

Heat sugar in heavy frying pan on medium until melted and dark brown in color, stirring often. Pour into ungreased 8 or 9 inch (20 or 22 cm) round casserole. Tilt dish to coat sides.

Beat eggs and condensed milk in medium bowl. Add evaporated milk and vanilla. Beat slowly until mixed. Pour over sugar. Set in 10 or 12 inch (25 cm or 30 cm) pan containing hot water no more than halfway up casserole. Bake in 350°F (175°C) oven for about 1 hour until a wooden pick inserted in center comes out clean. Cool. Chill for several hours or overnight. Run knife around outside edge. Put large plate over top. Invert quickly. Cuts into 8 wedges.

1 wedge: 315 Calories; 8.1 Total Fat; 143 mg Sodium; 11 g Protein; 51 g Carbohydrate; 0 g Dietary Fiber

Pictured on page 107.

Note: To make one caramel rose, soften six individual caramels. Place each on counter and sprinkle with granulated sugar. Press slightly with palm of hand. Roll flat. Shape each into a semicircle design. Roll one up tightly to form center of rose. Place remaining "petals" in a staggered fashion around center one.

SOPAIPILLAS

Dip these soh-pah-PEE-yahs into honey.

All-purpose flour	2 cups	500 mL
Skim milk powder	⅓ cup	75 mL
Baking powder	2 tsp.	10 mL
Salt	1 tsp.	5 mL
Hard margarine (or butter)	2 tbsp.	30 mL
Warm milk	1 cup	250 mL

Cooking oil, for deep-frying

Measure flour, skim milk powder, baking powder and salt into medium bowl. Stir. Cut in margarine until mixture is crumbly.

Add milk. Stir until dough forms a ball. Turn out onto lightly floured surface. Knead 8 to 10 times. Cover with tea towel. Let stand for 20 to 30 minutes. Roll out dough, ½ at a time, thinly as possible, on lightly floured surface. Cut into 3 inch (7.5 cm) squares.

Deep-fry, 2 or 3 at a time, in 375°F (190°C) cooking oil, turning and pushing beneath surface of cooking oil as they puff up and brown. Remove with slotted spoon to paper towels to drain. Makes about 32 sopaipillas.

1 sopaipilla: 66 Calories; 3.2 g Total Fat; 106 mg Sodium; 2 g Protein; 7 g Carbohydrate; trace Dietary Fiber

Pictured on page 72.

To prevent your custard from burning or boiling over while baking, place custard dish in a pan in which the water reaches only halfway up custard dish. This works well for any milk pudding.

glossary

Arroz Con Pollo (ah-ROHS con POH-yoh): Spanish for "rice with chicken;" also includes seasonings, tomatoes and green peppers.

Burrito (ber-EE-toh): Soft tortilla rolled or folded around filling such as meat, cheese, lettuce, tomatoes, peppers, sour cream and refried beans.

Calabacita (cah-lah-bah-SEE-tah): Spanish for "squash;" may be served with zucchini, corn, tomato sauce and onion.

Chilies Rellenos (CHEE-lehs ree-AY-nohs): Cheese-stuffed mild chili peppers which are then battered and deep fried.

Chili Con Carne (CHILL-ee kahn KAR-nee): Spanish for "chili with meat;" usually a ragout with cubed meat, onion and spices.

Chili Con Queso (CHILL-ee kahn-KAY-soh): Spanish for "chili with cheese;" a dip of melted cheese and mild green chili peppers served with tortilla chips or raw vegetables.

Chimichanga (chim-mee-CHAN-gah): Soft tortilla wrapped around filling of meat and vegetables, then deep-fried.

Chorizo (kor-EE-zoh): Spanish garlic sausage with red peppers made from different kinds of meat but usually pork or beef; can be sweet or spicy.

Empanada (em-pah-NAH-dah): Spanish pie or pastry filled with meat, fish or fruit and often eaten cold.

Enchilada — (en-chuh-LAH-dah): Soft tortilla rolled around meat or cheese filling, topped with tomato or chili sauce and usually baked.

Fajita (fah-HEE-tah): Steak, chicken or seafood marinated in seasonings and grilled with onions and sweet peppers; served wrapped in soft tortillas; usually served with tomato salsa, sour cream and guacamole.

Flan (FLAHN): Spanish custard, baked and covered with caramel.

Guacamole (gwah-kah-MOH-lee): Dip or sauce made with mashed avocado, lemon or lime juice and seasonings such as chili powder.

Jalapeño (hal-ah-PEN-yoh): Smooth dark green chili peppers which turn red when ripe; grow to about 2 inches long and up to 1 inch in diameter; easily seeded but gloves should be worn to protect the skin.

Mole (moh-LAY): Spicy sauce containing chocolate to add a hint of richness without being sweet.

Nacho (NAH-choh): Crisp baked or deep-fried tortilla chip.

Paella (pie-AY-yuh): Saffron-flavored rice dish with vegetables and chicken or shellfish with Spanish origins.

Picante (peh-CAHN-tay): Spanish for "spicy;" usually describes sauce.

Quesadilla (kay-sah-DEE-yah): Soft tortilla folded in half over filling such as meat, refried beans or vegetables; usually toasted and cut into wedges.

Salsa (SAHL-sah): Mexican sauce which can be spicy, mild or sweet; made from vegetables or fruits with seasonings.

Sopaipilla (soh-pah-PEE-yah): Deep-fried pastry, usually served with honey or syrup but sometimes served with toppings like refried beans.

Taco (TAH-koh): Folded sandwich made with a tortilla and fillings of beef, chicken and vegetables; usually the tortilla is crisp-fried, but some in some regions soft tortilla tacos are popular.

Tamale (tah-MAHL-ee): Filling of meat and vegetables coated with cornmeal dough and wrapped in a softened corn husk for steaming (the corn husk is not eaten).

Tortilla (tor-TEE-yah): Very thin, round flatbread made with wheat or corn flour; used to wrap around a filling or make into nacho chips.

Tostada (toh-STAH-dah): Open-faced sandwich on a crispy-fried tortilla with ingredients including beef or chicken, refried beans, vegetables, sour cream and guacamole.

Tostadito (toh-stah-DEE-toh): Individual tostada.

Mexican

glossary of beans

BEAN	COLOR	SIZE	SHAPE	DRIED	CANNED	COOKING TIME FOR DRIED
Black beans	Black	Medium	Oval	4	4	1-1½ hours
Black-eyed beans (Black-eyed peas)	Cream with black "eye"	Medium	Round	4	4	¾-1 hour
Chick peas (Garbanzo beans)	Cream	Medium-large	Acorn	4	4	1-2 hours
Fava beans (Broad beans)	Red-brown or green	Large or small	Broad	4	4	2 hours
Great northern beans (Haricot beans)	White	Medium-large	Oval	4	4	1-1½ hours
Kidney beans (Mexican beans)	Dark and light red	Large	Kidney-shaped	4	4	1-1½ hours
Lentils	Varied	Small	Narrow oval	4	4	¾ hour
Lima beans • Small (Butter beans Calico beans)	Pale white	Small	Thumbnail	4	4	1 hour
• Large	Cream	Large	Wide	4	4	1-1½ hours
Navy beans (White pea)	White	Small	Oval	4	4	1-1½ hours
Pinto beans	Pinkish brown mottled	Medium	Oval	4	4	1 hour
Soybeans (soya beans)	Tan or yellow	Large	Round	Soy sauce, soy milk, soybean oil, tofu		
Split peas (Field peas)	Green or yellow	Small	Round-split in ½	4	5	1¼-1½ hours

measurement tables

*T*hroughout this book measurements are given in Conventional and Metric measure. To compensate for differences between the two measurements due to rounding, a full metric measure is not always used. The cup used is the standard 8 fluid ounce. Temperature is given in degrees Fahrenheit and Celsius. Baking pan measurements are in inches and centimetres as well as quarts and litres. An exact metric conversion is given below as well as the working equivalent (Standard Measure).

OVEN TEMPERATURES

Fahrenheit (°F)	Celsius (°C)
175°	80°
200°	95°
225°	110°
250°	120°
275°	140°
300°	150°
325°	160°
350°	175°
375°	190°
400°	205°
425°	220°
450°	230°
475°	240°
500°	260°

PANS

Conventional Inches	Metric Centimetres
8x8 inch	20x20 cm
9x9 inch	22x22 cm
9x13 inch	22x33 cm
10x15 inch	25x38 cm
11x17 inch	28x43 cm
8x2 inch round	20x5 cm
9x2 inch round	22x5 cm
10x4^1/$_2$ inch tube	25x11 cm
8x4x3 inch loaf	20x10x7.5 cm
9x5x3 inch loaf	22x12.5x7.5 cm

CASSEROLES (CANADA & BRITAIN)

Standard Size Casserole	Exact Metric Measure
1 qt. (5 cups)	1.13 L
1^1/$_2$ qts. (7^1/$_2$ cups)	1.69 L
2 qts. (10 cups)	2.25 L
2^1/$_2$ qts. (12^1/$_2$ cups)	2.81 L
3 qts. (15 cups)	3.38 L
4 qts. (20 cups)	4.5 L
5 qts. (25 cups)	5.63 L

SPOONS

Conventional Measure	Metric Exact Conversion Millilitre (mL)	Metric Standard Measure Millilitre (mL)
1/8 teaspoon (tsp.)	0.6 mL	0.5 mL
1/4 teaspoon (tsp.)	1.2 mL	1 mL
1/2 teaspoon (tsp.)	2.4 mL	2 mL
1 teaspoon (tsp.)	4.7 mL	5 mL
2 teaspoons (tsp.)	9.4 mL	10 mL
1 tablespoon (tbsp.)	14.2 mL	15 mL

CUPS

1/4 cup (4 tbsp.)	56.8 mL	60 mL
1/3 cup (5^1/$_3$ tbsp.)	75.6 mL	75 mL
1/2 cup (8 tbsp.)	113.7 mL	125 mL
2/3 cup (10^2/$_3$ tbsp.)	151.2 mL	150 mL
3/4 cup (12 tbsp.)	170.5 mL	175 mL
1 cup (16 tbsp.)	227.3 mL	250 mL
4^1/$_2$ cups	1022.9 mL	1000 mL (1 L)

DRY MEASUREMENTS

Conventional Measure Ounces (oz.)	Metric Exact Conversion Grams (g)	Metric Standard Measure Grams (g)
1 oz.	28.3 g	28 g
2 oz.	56.7 g	57 g
3 oz.	85.0 g	85 g
4 oz.	113.4 g	125 g
5 oz.	141.7 g	140 g
6 oz.	170.1 g	170 g
7 oz.	198.4 g	200 g
8 oz.	226.8 g	250 g
16 oz.	453.6 g	500 g
32 oz.	907.2 g	1000 g (1 kg)

CASSEROLES (UNITED STATES)

Standard Size Casserole	Exact Metric Measure
1 qt. (4 cups)	900 mL
1^1/$_2$ qts. (6 cups)	1.35 L
2 qts. (8 cups)	1.8 L
2^1/$_2$ qts. (10 cups)	2.25 L
3 qts. (12 cups)	2.7 L
4 qts. (16 cups)	3.6 L
5 qts. (20 cups)	4.5 L

index

Company's Coming cookbooks are available at **retail locations** throughout Canada!

See mail order form

Buy any 2 cookbooks—choose a 3rd FREE of equal or less value than the lowest price paid.   *Available in French

Original Series — CA$14.99 Canada — US$10.99 USA & International

CODE		CODE		CODE	
SQ	150 Delicious Squares*	CT	Cooking For Two*	ODM	One-Dish Meals*
AP	Appetizers	DE	Desserts	PA	Pasta*
AC	Appliance Cooking*	KC	Kids Cooking*	PI	Pies*
BA	Barbecues*	LCA	Light Casseroles*	PZ	Pizza!*
BR	Breads*	LR	Light Recipes*	PR	Preserves*
BB	Breakfasts & Brunches*	LFC	Low-Fat Cooking*	SA	Salads*
CK	Cakes	LFP	Low-Fat Pasta*	SC	Slow Cooker Recipes*
CA	Casseroles*	MC	Main Courses	SS	Soups & Sandwiches
CH	Chicken, Etc.*	MAM	Make-Ahead Meals*	ST	Starters*
CFK	Cook For Kids **‹NEW›** (Aug 1, 2001)	ME	Meatless Cooking*	SF	Stir-Fry*
		MI	Microwave Cooking*	PB	The Potato Book*
CO	Cookies*	MU	Muffins & More*	VE	Vegetables

Greatest Hits — CA$12.99 Canada — US$9.99 USA & International

CODE		CODE		CODE	
BML	Biscuits, Muffins & Loaves*	MEX	Mexican*	SAW	Sandwiches & Wraps*
DSD	Dips, Spreads & Dressings*	ITAL	Italian*	SAS	Soups & Salads*

Lifestyle Series — CA$16.99 Canada — US$12.99 USA & International

CODE		CODE	
GR	Grilling*	LFP	Low-fat Pasta*
LFC	Low-fat Cooking*	DC	Diabetic Cooking*

Special Occasion Series — CA$19.99 Canada — US$19.99 USA & International

CODE	
CE	Chocolate Everything*

Company's Coming COOKBOOKS®

www.companyscoming.com
visit our web-site

COMPANY'S COMING PUBLISHING LIMITED
2311 - 96 Street
Edmonton, Alberta, Canada T6N 1G3
Tel: (780) 450-6223 Fax: (780) 450-1857

Mail Order Form

See reverse for list of cookbooks

EXCLUSIVE MAIL ORDER OFFER
Buy 2 Get 1 FREE!
Buy any 2 cookbooks—choose a **3rd FREE** of equal or less value than the lowest price paid.

QUANTITY	CODE	TITLE	PRICE EACH	PRICE TOTAL
			$	$

DON'T FORGET to indicate your FREE book(s). (see exclusive mail order offer above) PLEASE PRINT

	TOTAL BOOKS (including FREE)

TOTAL BOOKS PURCHASED: $

	INTERNATIONAL	CANADA & USA
Plus Shipping & Handling (PER DESTINATION)	$ 7.00 (one book)	$ 5.00 (1-3 books)
Additional Books (INCLUDING FREE BOOKS)	$ ($2.00 each)	$ ($1.00 each)
SUB-TOTAL	$	$
Canadian residents add G.S.T(7%)		$
TOTAL AMOUNT ENCLOSED	$	$

The Fine Print

- Orders outside Canada must be **PAID IN US FUNDS** by cheque or money order drawn on Canadian or US bank or by credit card.
- Make cheque or money order payable to: **COMPANY'S COMING PUBLISHING LIMITED.**
- Prices are expressed in Canadian dollars for Canada, US dollars for USA & International and are subject to change without prior notice.
- Orders are shipped surface mail. For courier rates, visit our web-site: **www.companyscoming.com** or contact us: **Tel: (780) 450-6223 Fax: (780) 450-1857.**
- Sorry, no C.O.D's.

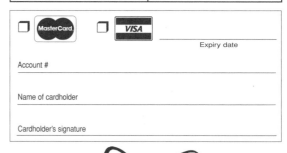

☐ MasterCard ☐ VISA

Expiry date _____

Account # _____

Name of cardholder _____

Cardholder's signature _____

Shipping Address

Send the cookbooks listed above to:

Name: _____

Street: _____

City: _____ Prov./State: _____

Country: _____ Postal Code/Zip: _____

Tel: (____) _____

E-mail address: _____

Gift Giving

- Let us help you with your gift giving!
- We will send cookbooks directly to the recipients of your choice if you give us their names and addresses.
- Please specify the titles you wish to send to each person.
- If you would like to include your personal note or card, we will be pleased to enclose it with your gift order.
- Company's Coming Cookbooks make excellent gifts: Birthdays, bridal showers, Mother's Day, Father's Day, graduation or any occasion... collect them all!